Ready® Common Core

2014

Mathematics Instruction **8**

Curriculum Associates

Project Manager: Pam Halloran
Revising Editor: Paul Meyers
Supervising Editor: Fran Fanning
Cover Designer and Illustrator: Julia Bourque
Book Design: Scott Hoffman

Table of Contents

Table of Contents

There are many ways to save time and energy when writing. We use initials like "TV" to stand for television or "PC" for personal computer. We use acronyms like SCUBA for "self contained underwater breathing apparatus." We even use notations like ". . ." when we don't want to continue a really long list.

In mathematics and science, there is a way to save time when writing really large or really small numbers. The Sun is approximately 150,000,000,000 meters, or 1.5×10^{11} meters, from the Earth. A small space on a computer chip is 0.000000035 or 3.5×10^{-8} meters. Using scientific notation is a much quicker way of dealing with numbers such as these.

In this unit, you will study how exponents are used in algebraic expressions as well as in scientific notation.

✓ Self Check

Before starting this unit, check off the skills you know below. As you complete each lesson, see how many more you can check off!

I can:	Before this unit	After this unit
simplify numerical expressions that include integer exponents, for example: $(5^8)(5^7) = 5^{15}$	☐	☐
solve equations of the form $p = x^2$ and $p = x^3$	☐	☐
evaluate square roots of perfect squares and cube roots of perfect cubes, for example: $\sqrt[3]{27} = 3$	☐	☐
write the repeating decimal equivalent to a rational number and the fraction equivalent to a repeating decimal, for example: $0.\overline{3} = \frac{1}{3}$	☐	☐
estimate the value of irrational numbers	☐	☐
use scientific notation to express very large or very small quantities and add, subtract, multiply, or divide with numbers expressed in scientific notation	☐	☐

Lesson 1   Part 1: Introduction 👥

Properties of Integer Exponents

CCSS
8.EE.A.1

In the past, you have written and evaluated expressions with exponents such as 5^3 and $x^2 + 1$. Now, take a look at this problem.

> Multiply: $(3^3)(3^4)$

🔍 Explore It

Use the math you know to answer the questions.

▪ What do the expressions (3^3) and (3^4) have in common? _____

▪ Write a multiplication expression without exponents that is equivalent to 3^3. _____

▪ How many factors of 3 did you write? _____

▪ Write a multiplication expression without exponents that is equivalent to 3^4. _____

▪ How many factors of 3 did you write? _____

▪ Write a multiplication expression without exponents that is equivalent to $(3^3)(3^4)$.

_____

▪ How many factors of 3 did you write? _____

▪ Write an expression with exponents to complete this equation: $(3^3)(3^4) =$ _____

▪ What is the relationship between the exponents of the factors and the exponent of the product in your equation?

_____

▪ Use words to explain how to multiply $(3^3)(3^4)$.

_____

_____

You have seen one example of how to multiply powers with the same base. Here are two more:

$$(5^8)(5^5) = 5 \cdot 5 \cdot 5 \cdot 5 \cdot 5 \cdot 5 \cdot 5 \cdot 5 \cdot 5 \cdot 5 \cdot 5 \cdot 5 \cdot 5 = 5^{8+5} = 5^{13}$$

$$(x^6)(x^2) = x \cdot x \cdot x \cdot x \cdot x \cdot x \cdot x \cdot x = x^{6+2} = x^8$$

In general, for the product of powers with the same base $(n^a)(n^b) = n^{a+b}$, where $n \neq 0$.

You can also use the meaning of exponents to divide powers with the same base.

Divide $\frac{4^{12}}{4^5}$.

$$\frac{4^{12}}{4^5} = \frac{4 \cdot 4 \cdot 4 \cdot 4 \cdot 4 \cdot 4 \cdot 4 \cdot 4 \cdot 4 \cdot 4 \cdot 4 \cdot 4}{4 \cdot 4 \cdot 4 \cdot 4 \cdot 4} \qquad 4^{12} \text{ is twelve 4s multiplied together.}$$

$$= \frac{4}{4} \cdot \frac{4}{4} \cdot \frac{4}{4} \cdot \frac{4}{4} \cdot \frac{4}{4} \cdot 4 \cdot 4 \cdot 4 \cdot 4 \cdot 4 \cdot 4 \cdot 4 \qquad 4^5 \text{ is five 4s multiplied together.}$$

$$= 1 \cdot 1 \cdot 1 \cdot 1 \cdot 1 \cdot 4 \cdot 4 \cdot 4 \cdot 4 \cdot 4 \cdot 4 \cdot 4 \qquad \text{Any non-zero number divided by itself is 1.}$$

$$= 4 \cdot 4 \cdot 4 \cdot 4 \cdot 4 \cdot 4 \cdot 4 \qquad \text{Seven 4s multiplied together is } 4^7.$$

$$= 4^7$$

So, $\frac{4^{12}}{4^5} = 4^7$. What is the relationship between the exponents of the dividend, divisor, and quotient? The exponent of the quotient is the exponent of the dividend minus the exponent of the divisor. $12 - 5 = 7$.

In general, for the quotient of two powers with the same base, $\frac{n^a}{n^b} = n^{a-b}$, where $n \neq 0$.

✏️ **Reflect**

1 Explain why $\frac{5^{10}}{5^2}$ equals 5^8.

_____

_____

_____

_____

Read the problem below. Then explore how to find the product of powers with the same base *and* the same exponent.

Simplify: $(3^2)^4$

🔍 Model It

You can write it another way.

$(3^2)^4 =$ means *3 squared, multiplied as a factor 4 times.*

$(3^2)^4 = 3^2 \cdot 3^2 \cdot 3^2 \cdot 3^2$

$(3^2)^4$ is the product of 4 powers, each with the same base (3) and the same exponent (2).

🔍 Solve It

You can apply the associative property of multiplication.

$(3^2)^4 = 3^2 \cdot 3^2 \cdot 3^2 \cdot 3^2$ $(3^2)^4$ is the product of four 3^2s multiplied together.

$\quad = (3^2 \cdot 3^2)(3^2 \cdot 3^2)$ Apply the associative property of multiplication.

$\quad = (3^4)(3^4)$ This is the product of powers with the same bases.

$\quad = 3^{4+4}$ Add the exponents.

$\quad = 3^8$

Connect It

Now you will explore the concept from the previous page further.

2 Simplify: $(3^2)^4 = $ _____

3 Describe the relationship between the exponents of $(3^2)^4$ and the exponent of 3^8.

_____

4 Complete these examples of products of powers that have the same base and the same exponent.

$(5^8)^6 = 5^8 \cdot 5^8 \cdot 5^8 \cdot 5^8 \cdot 5^8 \cdot 5^8 = 5^{8+8+8+8+8+8} = 5^{8 \cdot 6} = $ _____

$(953^7)^3 = 953^7 \cdot 953^7 \cdot 953^7 = 953^{7+7+7} = 953^{7 \cdot 3} = $ _____

5 In general, for a product of powers that have the same base and the same exponent, $(n^a)^b = $ _____, where $n \neq 0$.

Now look at how to simplify a product of powers when the bases are *different* and the exponents are the same.

Simplify: $(2^3)(4^3)$

6 Write an expression without exponents that is equivalent to $(2^3)(4^3)$. _____

7 Apply the associative and commutative properties of multiplication to write your expression as the product of groups of $2 \cdot 4$. _____

8 How many groups of $2 \cdot 4$ do you multiply together to get $(2^3)(4^3)$? _____

9 Complete this equation: $(2^3)(4^3) = (2 \times 4)^{\boxed{}} = \boxed{}^3$

10 In general, for a product of powers that have different bases and the same exponent, $(a^n)(b^n) = $ _____, where $a \neq 0$ and $b \neq 0$.

Try It

Use what you just learned to solve these problems. Write your answers using exponents.

11 Simplify: $(2^{18})^8 = $ _____

12 Simplify: $(4^9)(25^9) = $ _____, or _____

Read the problem below. Then explore simplifying expressions with exponents equal to zero.

Simplify: 5^0

Model It

You can write it another way.

It doesn't make sense to ask yourself, "What is zero 5s multiplied together?" We will need to approach this problem another way.

So far, you have worked with powers where the exponents are counting numbers (1, 2, 3, . . .). The rules for working with powers are the same when the exponent is 0.

You have seen that when you multiply powers with bases that are the same you add the exponents.

$$(5^0)(5^4) = 5^{0+4} = 5^4$$

Solve It

You can apply the identity property of multiplication.

You know that 1 times any expression is equivalent to that expression by the identity property of multiplication.

$$(1)(5^4) = 5^4$$

Because $(1)(5^4) = 5^4$

and $(5^0)(5^4) = 5^4$,

5^0 must therefore be equal to 1.

Connect It

Now you will explore the concept from the previous page further.

13 Simplify: $5^0 =$ _____

14 Complete these examples:

$12^0 =$ _____

_____ $= 1$

$(-7)^0 =$ _____

15 In general, for a power where the exponent is equal to 0, $n^0 =$ _____, where $n \neq 0$.

The rules for products of powers also apply when the exponent is a negative integer.

16 Complete this equation: $(6^5)(6^{-5}) = 6^{\boxed{}} =$ _____

17 You already know that a number times its reciprocal equals 1. For example, $3 \cdot \dfrac{1}{3} = \dfrac{3}{3} = 1$.

Now complete this equation: $6^5 \cdot \dfrac{1}{6^5} =$ _____ $=$ _____

18 Since $6^5 \cdot 6^{-5} =$ _____ and $6^5 \cdot \dfrac{1}{6^5} =$ _____ , then $6^{-5} =$ _____.

19 Complete these examples:

$10^{-6} =$ _____

$(-34)^{-7} =$ _____

_____ $= \dfrac{1}{142^{13}}$

20 In general, for a power where the exponent is a negative integer, $n^{-a} =$ _____,

where $n \neq 0$.

Try It

Use what you just learned to solve these problems. Write your answers using exponents where appropriate.

21 Simplify: $455^0 =$ _____

22 Simplify: $19^{-4} =$ _____

Study the student model below. Then solve problems 23–25.

In this problem, you have to apply more than one rule of working with exponents.

Student Model

Simplify: $2^4 \cdot 2^{-7}$

Look at how you could show your work.

$2^4 \cdot 2^{-7}$ product of powers with equivalent bases

$= 2^{4+(-7)}$ add exponents

$= 2^{-3}$ power with a negative integer exponent

$= \dfrac{1}{2^3}$ reciprocal with positive exponent

Solution: $2^4 \cdot 2^{-7} = \dfrac{1}{2^3}$

Pair/Share

If x and a are counting numbers, is x^{-a} less than or greater than 1? Explain.

Remember the order of operations. Simplify the expression within the parentheses first.

23 Simplify: $\left(3^2 \cdot 4^2\right)^5$

Show your work.

Pair/Share

Does $5^9 \cdot 6^7 = (30)^{16}$? Justify your answer.

Solution: _____

24 Simplify: $9^{-8} \cdot \frac{1}{9^3}$. Write your answer with a positive exponent.

Show your work.

Solution: _____

25 Which expression is equivalent to $\frac{45^{-3}}{45^3}$?

A 45^{-1}

B 45^0

C $\frac{1}{45^6}$

D 45^6

Isaac chose **A** as the correct answer. How did he get that answer?

_____

_____

_____

_____

Solve the problems.

1 Which expression is equivalent to $(-4^{-5})^0$?

    A   1

    B $(-4)^5$

    C $\dfrac{1}{(-4)^5}$

    D $\dfrac{1^5}{-4}$

2 Which expression is equivalent to $\dfrac{(7^2)^5}{7^{-6}}$?

    A   7

    B 7^4

    C 7^{13}

    D 7^{16}

3 Which expression is equivalent to $\dfrac{1}{49}$? Select all that apply.

    A $7^{-1} \times 7^{-1}$

    B $7^8 \times 7^{-6}$

    C $7^{-5} \times 7^3$

    D $7^7 \times 7^{-9}$

    E $7^{-2} \times 7^4$

4 Write 16^8 as a power with a base of 4.

_____

5 Look at the equations below. Choose True or False for each equation.

A $2^4 \times 3^4 = 4^6$ ☐ True ☐ False

B $5^2 \div 5^3 = \dfrac{1}{5}$ ☐ True ☐ False

C $(6^3)^4 = (6^4)^3$ ☐ True ☐ False

D $\dfrac{3^2}{3^7} = 3^2 \times 3^{-7}$ ☐ True ☐ False

E $\dfrac{8^0}{8^{-4}} = 8^{-4}$ ☐ True ☐ False

F $4^{10} \div 4^5 = 4^2$ ☐ True ☐ False

6 Write each of these numbers as the product of a whole number and a power of 10. Then describe the relationship between place value and exponents.

$3{,}000 =$ _____

$300 =$ _____

$30 =$ _____

$3 =$ _____

$0.3 =$ _____

$0.03 =$ _____

$0.003 =$ _____

_____

_____

_____

_____

✓ **Self Check** *Go back and see what you can check off on the Self Check on page 1.*

Lesson 2 Part 1: Introduction 👥

Square Roots and Cube Roots

In Lesson 1 you learned the properties of integer exponents. Now, take a look at this problem.

> The length of each side of a square measures s inches long. The area of the square is 49 in.² What is the length of one side of the square?

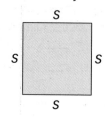

🔍 Explore It

Use the math you know to answer the question.

- Describe in words how to find the area of the square given that each side is *s* inches long.

  _____

- Write a multiplication expression using the variable *s* to represent the area of the square.

  _____

- Write an expression using the variable *s* and an exponent to represent the area of the square. _____

- Write an equation setting your expression equal to the area of the square given in the problem. _____

- Consider the factors of 49. Explain what the two sides of the equation have in common when you write each as the product of two factors.

  _____

Find Out More

The number 49 is one of a set of numbers called perfect squares. A perfect square is a number that results from multiplying an integer by itself. The first 15 square numbers are shown.

$1^2 = 1$	$4^2 = 16$	$7^2 = 49$	$10^2 = 100$	$13^2 = 169$
$2^2 = 4$	$5^2 = 25$	$8^2 = 64$	$11^2 = 121$	$14^2 = 196$
$3^2 = 9$	$6^2 = 36$	$9^2 = 81$	$12^2 = 144$	$15^2 = 225$

Look at the equation you wrote on the previous page, $s^2 = 49$. How do you solve an equation where a variable squared is equivalent to a perfect square? You have solved equations before by using inverse operations. You solved addition equations by subtracting. You solved division equations by multiplying. What is the inverse operation of squaring a number?

The inverse operation of squaring is finding the **square root**. A square root of a number is any number that you can multiply by itself to get your original number. For example, 3 is a square root of 9, because $3 \cdot 3 = 9$. Another square root of 9 is -3, because $(-3) \cdot (-3) = 9$.

The symbol $\sqrt{}$ means *positive square root*. So, $\sqrt{9} = 3$.

$s^2 = 49$	The inverse of squaring is finding a square root.
$\sqrt{s^2} = \sqrt{49}$	Find the square root of both sides.
$\sqrt{s^2} = \sqrt{7^2}$	49 is a perfect square.
$s = 7$	The length of one side of the square is 7 inches.

Reflect

1 What is the difference between dividing 16 by 2 and finding the square roots of 16?

_____

_____

_____

_____

Read the problem below. Then explore how to solve equations with cubes and cube roots.

Each edge of a cube measures a feet long. The volume of the cube is 125 ft^3. What is the measure of each edge of the cube?

Picture It

Draw and label the cube.

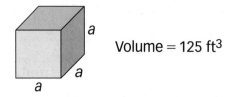

Volume $= 125$ ft^3

The length, width, and height of the cube each measure a feet.

Solve It

You can apply the formula for the volume of a cube.

The volume of the cube is the product of its length, width, and height.

$$a \cdot a \cdot a = V \quad \text{length} = a, \text{width} = a, \text{and height} = a$$

$$a^3 = V \quad \text{Substitute the given volume of the cube for } V.$$

$$a^3 = 125$$

You can use this equation to find the value of a.

Connect It

Now you will solve the problem from the previous page.

2 Complete the prime factorization of 125.

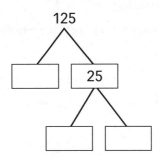

3 Write 125 as the product of three factors. _____

4 Write 125 as a power of base 5. _____

5 What does 125 have in common with a^3 when 125 is written as a power? _____

The product of an integer multiplied together three times is a **perfect cube**. Finding the **cube root** is the inverse of cubing a number. The cube root of a number is the number that is multiplied together three times to produce the original number. The symbol $\sqrt[3]{}$ means *find the cube root.*

6 Look at Solve It on the previous page. The equation shows a variable cubed equal to a perfect cube. Use the cube root to complete the solution.

$$a^3 = 125$$
$$\sqrt[3]{a^3} = \sqrt[3]{\boxed{}}$$
$$\sqrt[3]{a^3} = \sqrt[3]{\boxed{}}$$

Solution: Each edge of the cube is _____ feet long.   _____ = _____

Try It

Use what you just learned to solve these problems. Show your work on a separate sheet of paper.

7 Solve: $y^3 = 8$ _____

8 Solve: $x^3 = 27$ _____

Read the problem below. Then explore how to use square roots and cube roots to solve word problems.

City Park is a square piece of land with an area of 10,000 square yards. What is the length of the fence that encloses the park?

Picture It

You can draw a diagram to help solve the problem.

The park is a square. The fence runs along the outside edge of the park.

Area = 10,000 yd²

City park

Fence

The length of the fence is the perimeter of the square.

Solve It

To find the perimeter of the square park, you need to know the length of one side of the square.

Let f be the length of one side of the square.

$A = 10,000$ Area of the park is 10,000 yd²

$f^2 = 10,000$ Area equals the length of one side squared.

Connect It

Now you will solve the problem from the previous page.

9 What number squared equals 10,000? _____

10 Look at Solve It on the previous page. Solve the equation for *f*.

$$f^2 = 10,000$$

_____

_____

_____

11 What is the length of each side of the park? _____

12 Write and solve an equation to find the perimeter of the park. _____

13 What is the length of the fence that encloses the park? _____

14 The park's rectangular garden area is 450 square yards. Its length is twice its width. Find the dimensions of the garden. Begin with the equation $(2w)(w) = 450$.

Rewrite the equation using exponents. _____

Divide both sides by 2. _____

Solve and write the garden's dimensions. _____

Try It

Use what you just learned about square roots and cube roots to solve these problems.

15 The volume of a cube is 1,000 cm^3. What is the length of an edge? _____

16 A gift box in the shape of a cube has a volume of 216 cm^3. What is the area of the base of the box? _____

17 A scientist finds the temperature of a sample at the beginning of an experiment is $t°C$. After 1 hour, the temperature is $t^2°C$. If the temperature after 1 hour is 81°C, what are two possible original temperatures? What is the difference between the possible original temperatures? _____

Study the student model below. Then solve problems 18–20.

In this problem, you will divide before you find the square root.

Student Model

The distance in feet that a freely falling dropped object falls in t seconds is given by the equation $\frac{d}{16} = t^2$.

How long does it take a dropped object to fall 64 feet?

Look at how you could solve this problem.

The given equation is: $\frac{d}{16} = t^2$

Substitute 64 for d: $\frac{64}{16} = t^2$

Simplify: $4 = t^2$

Take the square root of both sides: $\sqrt{4} = \sqrt{t^2}$

$t = 2$

Solution: ___The object takes 2 seconds to fall 64 feet.___

Pair/Share

How far does an object fall in 1 second?

What information do you need to calculate the volume of a cube?

18 The area of the top face of a cube is 9 square meters. What is the volume of the cube?

Show your work.

Pair/Share

The cube has 6 faces. What does the expression 6 · 9 describe?

Solution: _____

19 The length of each side of a cube is x centimeters. If x is an integer, why can't the volume of the cube equal 15 cm^3?

Show your work.

Write an equation showing a variable expression for volume is equal to 15.

Solution: _____

_____

_____

Pair/Share

Are all perfect cubes also multiples of 3? Are all multiples of 3 also perfect cubes? Discuss.

20 Yesterday, there were b milligrams of bacteria in a lab experiment. Today, there are b^2 milligrams of bacteria. If there are 400 milligrams today, how many milligrams of bacteria were there yesterday?

A 20 milligrams

B 200 milligrams

C 1,600 milligrams

D 160,000 milligrams

Eva chose **B** as the correct answer. How did she get that answer?

_____

_____

_____

Do you square a number or find the square root to solve the problem?

Pair/Share

Talk about the problem and then write your answer together.

Solve the problems.

1   Solve $a^3 = 64$.

    A $a = 4$

    B $a = 8$

    C $a = 21$

    (D) $a = 32$

2   Which number is a perfect square?

    A   8

    B   18

    C   200

    (D)   225

3   The fractions below are the values of x in the given equations. Write the correct fraction inside the box for each equation.

$\frac{9}{8}$	$\frac{1}{2}$	$\frac{3}{4}$	$\frac{2}{3}$

    A $x^2 = \dfrac{4}{9}$ $\boxed{\dfrac{2}{3}}$

    B $x^3 = \dfrac{27}{64}$ $\boxed{\dfrac{3}{4}}$

    C $x^2 = \dfrac{81}{64}$ $\boxed{\dfrac{9}{8}}$

    D $x^3 = \dfrac{1}{8}$ $\boxed{\dfrac{1}{2}}$

4 Use the numbers shown to make the two equations true. Each number can be used only once. Write the number in the appropriate box for each equation.

| 3 | 6 | 100 | 36 | 1,000 | 1,000,000 |

(handwritten work:)
$$\frac{100}{10\overline{)1000}}$$
$$\begin{array}{cc} 36 & 36 \\ \wedge & \wedge \\ 9\ 4 & 6\ 6 \\ \wedge\ \wedge & \wedge\ \wedge \\ 3\ 3\ 2\ 2 & 3\ 2\ 3\ 2 \end{array}$$

$$10\sqrt{\boxed{6 \cdot 6}} = \boxed{36} \qquad \sqrt[3]{\boxed{10 \cdot 10 \cdot 10}} = \boxed{1000}$$

$$6\overline{)36}$$

5 If x is a positive integer, is $\sqrt{\dfrac{1}{x^2}}$ greater than, less than, or equivalent to $\sqrt[3]{\dfrac{1}{x^3}}$?

Show your work.

$$\sqrt{\frac{1}{x^2}} \qquad \sqrt[3]{\frac{1}{x^3}}$$

$$\sqrt{\frac{1}{x \cdot x}} > \sqrt{\frac{1}{x \cdot x \cdot x}} \qquad \frac{1}{x} \cdot \frac{1}{x} \cdot \frac{1}{x}$$

Answer $\underline{\sqrt{\frac{1}{x^2}} \text{ is less than } \sqrt[3]{\frac{1}{x^3}} \text{ because one has only two sicles and}}$
$\underline{\sqrt[3]{\frac{1}{x^3}} \text{ has more than two measurements.}}$

6 Describe how you could use inverse operations to solve the equation $\sqrt{x} = 4$.

(handwritten:) $x \cdot \sqrt{x} = \sqrt[2]{4} \qquad \boxed{x = 2}$

$\underline{\text{You use inverse operation to solve the equation because}}$
$\underline{\text{you taking the cube root of the number.}}$

(handwritten work:)
$$\begin{array}{c} 4 \\ \wedge \\ 2\ 2 \end{array} \qquad \sqrt[2]{x} = x = \sqrt[2]{4}$$
$$\sqrt{x \cdot x} \qquad \boxed{x = 2}$$

✓ **Self Check** *Go back and see what you can check off on the Self Check on page 1.*

What are rational numbers?

Rational numbers are numbers that can be written as the quotient of two integers. Since the bar in a fraction represents division, every fraction whose numerator and denominator is an integer is a rational number.

Any number that *could* be written as a fraction whose numerator and denominator is an integer is also a rational number.

🔍 **Think**   Every integer, whole number, and natural number is a rational number.

You can write every integer, whole number, and natural number as a fraction. So they are all rational numbers. The square root of a perfect square is also a rational number.

$3 = \dfrac{3}{1}$

$-5 = \dfrac{5}{1}$

$0 = \dfrac{0}{1}$

$\sqrt{25} = 5$ or $\dfrac{5}{1}$

🔍 **Think**   Every terminating decimal is a rational number.

You can write every terminating decimal as a fraction. So terminating decimals are all rational numbers.

You can use what you know about place value to find the fraction that is equivalent to any terminating decimal.

0.4	*four tenths*	$\dfrac{4}{10} = \dfrac{2}{5}$
0.75	*seventy-five hundredths*	$\dfrac{75}{100} = \dfrac{3}{4}$
0.386	*three hundred eighty-six thousandths*	$\dfrac{386}{1,000} = \dfrac{193}{500}$
$\sqrt{0.16} = 0.4$	*four tenths*	$\dfrac{4}{10} = \dfrac{2}{5}$

🔍 Think Every repeating decimal is a rational number.

You can write every repeating decimal as a fraction.
So repeating decimals are all rational numbers.

As an example, look at the repeating decimal $0.\overline{3}$.

You can write and solve an equation to find a fraction equivalent to a repeating decimal.

Let $x = 0.\overline{3}$

$10 \cdot x = 10 \cdot 0.\overline{3}$ The repeating pattern goes to the
                    tenths place. Multiply both
$10x = 3.\overline{3}$ sides by 10.

$10x - x = 3.\overline{3} - 0.\overline{3}$ Subtract x from the left side and $0.\overline{3}$ from the right side.

$9x = 3$ The equation is still balanced because x and $0.\overline{3}$ are equivalent.

$\dfrac{9x}{9} = \dfrac{3}{9}$

$x = \dfrac{3}{9} \text{ or } \dfrac{1}{3}$

$0.\overline{3} = \dfrac{1}{3}$

Here's another example of how you can write a repeating decimal as a fraction.

$x = 0.\overline{512}$

$1{,}000x = 512.\overline{512}$ The repeating pattern goes to the thousandths place.
                    Multiply by 1,000.

$1{,}000x - x = 512.\overline{512} - 0.\overline{512}$ Subtract x from the left side and the repeating decimal
                    from the right side.

$999x = 512$

$x = \dfrac{512}{999}$

✏️ Reflect

1 What fraction is equivalent to 5.1? Is 5.1 a rational number? Explain.

_____

_____

_____

Explore It

What numbers are not rational? Let's look at a number like $\sqrt{2}$, the square root of a number that is not a perfect square.

2 Look at the number line below. The number $\sqrt{2}$ is between $\sqrt{1}$ and $\sqrt{4}$. Since $\sqrt{1} = 1$ and $\sqrt{4} = 2$, that means that $\sqrt{2}$ must be between what two integers?

_____

3 Draw a point on the number line where you would locate $\sqrt{2}$. Where did you draw the point? _____

4 Calculate: $1.3^2 =$ _____ $1.4^2 =$ _____ $1.5^2 =$ _____

5 Based on your calculations, draw a point on the number line below where you would locate $\sqrt{2}$ now. Where did you draw the point? _____

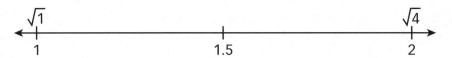

6 Calculate: $1.41^2 =$ _____ $1.42^2 =$ _____

7 Based on these calculations, $\sqrt{2}$ is between which two decimals? _____

8 You can continue to estimate, getting closer and closer to the value of $\sqrt{2}$. For example, $1.414^2 = 1.999396$ and $1.415^2 = 2.002225$, but you will never find an exact number that multiplied by itself equals 2. The decimal will also never have a repeating pattern.

$\sqrt{2}$ cannot be expressed as a terminating or repeating decimal, so it cannot be written as a fraction. Numbers like $\sqrt{2}$ and $\sqrt{5}$ are not rational. You can only estimate their values. They are called **irrational numbers.** Here, *irrational* means "cannot be set as a ratio." The set of rational and irrational numbers together make up the set of **real numbers.**

Now try this problem.

9 The value π is a decimal that does not repeat and does not terminate. Is it a rational or irrational number? Explain.

_____

_____

💬 Talk About It

You can estimate the value of an irrational number like $\sqrt{5}$ and locate that value on a number line.

10 $\sqrt{5}$ is between which two integers? Explain your reasoning.

_____

11 Mark a point at an approximate location for $\sqrt{5}$ on the number line below. $\sqrt{5}$ is between which two decimals to the tenths place? _____

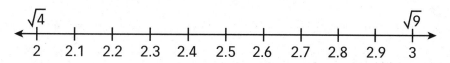

12 Calculate: $2.22^2 =$ _____ $2.23^2 =$ _____ $2.24^3 =$ _____
Based on your results, $\sqrt{5}$ is between which two decimals to the hundredths place?
_____

13 Draw a number line from 2.2 to 2.3. Label tick marks at tenths to show 2.21, 2.22, 2.23, and so on. Mark a point at the approximate location of $\sqrt{5}$ to the hundredths place.

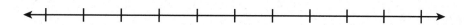

✏️ Try It Another Way

Explore using a calculator to estimate irrational numbers.

14 Enter $\sqrt{5}$ on a calculator and press Enter. What is the result on your screen? _____

15 If this number is equal to $\sqrt{5}$, then the number squared should equal _____.

16 Clear your calculator. Then enter your result from problem 14. Square the number. What is the result on your screen? _____

17 Explain this result.

_____

_____

Connect It

Talk through these problems as a class, then write your answers below.

18 Illustrate: Show that $0.\overline{74}$ is equivalent to a fraction. Is $0.\overline{74}$ a rational or irrational number? Explain.

_____

_____

_____

_____

_____

_____

_____

_____

19 Analyze: A circle has a circumference of 3π inches. Is it possible to state the exact length of the circumference as a decimal? Explain.

_____

_____

20 Create: Draw a Venn diagram showing the relationships among the following sets of numbers: integers, irrational numbers, natural numbers, rational numbers, real numbers, and whole numbers.

Put It Together

Use what you have learned to complete this task.

21 Consider these numbers:

$\sqrt{50}$ $3.4\overline{56}$ 0 $\sqrt{\dfrac{4}{9}}$ 0.38 $\sqrt{81}$ 2π $\sqrt{1.69}$ $\sqrt{\dfrac{2}{9}}$

A Write each of the numbers in the list above in the correct box.

Rational Numbers	Irrational Numbers

B Circle one of the numbers you said was rational. Explain how you decided that the number was rational.

_____

_____

C Now circle one of the numbers you said was irrational. Explain how you decided that the number was irrational.

_____

_____

D Draw a number line and locate the two numbers you circled on the line. Write a comparison statement using <, =, or > to compare the numbers.

_____

Lesson 4   Part 1: Introduction

Scientific Notation

You've learned about place value and investigated multiplying and dividing by powers of 10. Now, take a look at this problem.

> The planet Venus is more than 60,000,000 miles from the Sun. Write this number as the product of two factors:
>
> (a number greater than or equal to 1 but less than 10) $\times$ (a power of 10)

🔍 Explore It

Use the math you already know to solve the problem.

- Write 60,000,000 in words. _____

- Fill in the missing factor: $60,000,000 = 6 \cdot$ _____

- Write the second factor in the equation as a product of 10s.

  _____

- Write the second factor as a power of 10. Explain your reasoning.

  _____

- Explain how you could write 60,000,000 as the product of a number greater than or

  equal to 1 that is multiplied by a power of 10. _____

  _____

Find Out More

Scientists often work with very large numbers, such as the distance from Venus to the Sun or the number of cells in a human body. Writing and calculating with very large numbers can be tedious and inconvenient.

When you wrote 60,000,000 as 6×10^7, you used **scientific notation**. Scientific notation uses exponents to make it easier to work with very large or very small numbers. To write a number using scientific notation, write it as a product of two factors:

To write the number 1,850,000 in scientific notation,

$$1,850,000 = 1850000$$

Move the decimal point to get a number between 1 and 10.

$$= 1.85 \times 10^6$$

The power of 10 is equal to the number of place values that the digits increase.

The power doesn't tell you the number of zeros in your answer. Rather, it tells you how many place values the digits increase.

To write the number 3.54×10^5 in standard form, we move each digit in 3.54 up 5 place values because we are multiplying by 10^5.

$$3.54 \times 10^5 = 3.54000 = 354,000$$

To translate between scientific notation and standard notation, change the place values of the digits according to the power of 10.

Reflect

1 Write 6.85×10^8 in standard form. Show your work.

_____

_____

_____

Read the problem below. Then explore how to write very small numbers using scientific notation.

Seven nanoseconds is equivalent to 7 one-billionths of a second, or 0.000000007 second. Write 0.000000007 in scientific notation.

🔍 Picture It

Look at the patterns in the chart below.

100	$10 \cdot 10$	10^2
10	10	10^1
1	1	10^0
0.1	$\dfrac{1}{10} = \dfrac{1}{10^1}$	10^{-1}
0.01	$\dfrac{1}{10 \cdot 10} = \dfrac{1}{10^2}$	10^{-2}
0.001	$\dfrac{1}{10 \cdot 10 \cdot 10} = \dfrac{1}{10^3}$	10^{-3}
0.0001	$\dfrac{1}{10 \cdot 10 \cdot 10 \cdot 10} = \dfrac{1}{10^4}$	10^{-4}

🔍 Model It

You can write the decimal as a fraction.

$$0.000000007 = \frac{7}{1,000,000,000}$$

$$= 7 \cdot \frac{1}{1,000,000,000}$$

🔍 Solve It

You can write the number as the product of a number that is greater than or equal to 1 but less than 10. When you multiply by a number by a power of 10, the decimal point moves to the right, or the place value of each digit moves up.

0.000000007   Move the decimal point 9 places to the right.

Connect It

Now look at different ways to solve the problem.

2 Write 1,000,000,000 as a product of 10s. _____

3 Write 1,000,000,000 as a power of 10. _____

4 Look at the table on the previous page. Write $\frac{1}{1,000,000,000}$ as 10 to a power to complete

the equation: $7 \cdot \frac{1}{1,000,000,000} =$ _____ $\times$ _____

5 Look at Solve It. When you have to move the decimal point to the right to express a
number in scientific notation, will the power of 10 be positive or negative? _____

6 When a number is written in scientific notation, a _____ exponent means the
number is greater than 1 and a _____ exponent means the number is between
0 and 1.

7 Is 2.14×10^{-5} greater than 1 or between 0 and 1? Explain.

_____

8 Write $2.14 \cdot 10^{-5}$ in standard form.

$2.14 \times 10^{-5} = \frac{214}{100} \times \frac{1}{10^5}$

$= $ _____

$= $ _____

9 Explain how to write $2.14 \cdot 10^{-5}$ in standard form by moving the decimal point.

_____

Try It

Use what you just learned to solve these problems. Show your work.

10 Write 63,120,000 in scientific notation. _____

11 Write 9.054×10^{-6} in standard form. _____

Read the problem below. Then explore how to compare numbers written in scientific notation.

> Earth is about 1.5×10^8 kilometers from the Sun, while the planet Neptune is almost 4.5×10^9 kilometers from the Sun. The distance from Neptune to Earth is about how many times the distance from the Sun to Earth?

Model It

You can write the distances of the planets from the Sun in standard form and compare them.

1.5×10^8 kilometers = 150,000,000 kilometers

4.5×10^9 kilometers = 4,500,000,000 kilometers

To find how many times as great 4,500,000,000 is than 150,000,000, divide.

4,500,000,000 ÷ 150,000,000

Model It

You can compare the distances of the planets from the Sun using scientific notation.

To compare 1.5×10^8 and 4.5×10^9:

First, compare 1.5 and 4.5.

4.5 is how many times as great as 1.5?

Then, compare 10^8 and 10^9.

10^9 is how many times as great as 10^8?

Connect It

Now you will solve the problem using standard form and scientific notation.

12 Look at the first Model It on the previous page. 4,500,000,000 is how many times the value of 150,000,000?

_____

13 Look at the second Model It. 4.5 is how many times the value of 1.5? Explain your reasoning.

_____

14 10^9 is how many times the value of 10^8? Explain your reasoning.

_____

15 Look at your answers to problems 13 and 14. 4.5×10^9 is how many times the value of 1.5×10^8? Give your answer in both scientific notation and standard form.

_____

16 Which method of comparing the numbers would you use? Explain.

_____

_____

Try It

Use what you just learned to solve these problems. Show your work on a separate sheet of paper.

17 6×10^{-5} is how many times the value of 3×10^{-8}? _____

18 Star A is about 3.4×10^{18} miles from Earth. Star B is 6.8×10^{16} miles from Earth. Star A is how many times as far from Earth as Star B? _____

Study the student model below. Then solve problems 19–21.

The student moved the decimal point the number of places necessary to get a number greater than or equal to 1 and less than 10.

Student Model

Write 0.0000408306 in scientific notation.

Look at how you could solve this problem.

In scientific notation, the solution will look like $n \cdot 10^a$. n must be greater than or equal to 1 and less than 10. a must be an integer.

To write 0.0000408306 in scientific notation, first move the decimal point 5 places to the right. Then multiply that number by a power of 10. The exponent in that power of 10 will be negative -5, which is found by counting the number of places the decimal is moved to the right.

Solution: $\underline{0.0000408306 = 4.08306 \times 10^{-5}}$

💬 Pair/Share

What is another method you could use to write the number in scientific notation?

Do you move the exponent to the right or to the left to write the number in scientific notation.

19 The mass of Earth is about 5,974,000,000,000,000,000,000,000 kilograms. Write this number in scientific notation.

Show your work.

💬 Pair/Share

Explain why the procedure used to write a number in scientific notation works.

Solution: _____

20 Use the information in the table to solve the problem.

Orbiting Body	Approximate Distance from the Sun (in miles)
Mercury	36,300,000
Mars	142,000,000
Neptune	2,800,000,000
Pluto	3,670,000,000

Show your work.

Write each distance in scientific notation.

Mercury _____

Mars _____

Neptune _____

Pluto _____

Neptune is about how many times as far from the Sun as Mars is from the Sun?

Solution: _____

_____

_____

Will the exponent be positive or negative?

🗨 Pair/Share

How does writing numbers in scientific notation make numbers easier to work with?

21 Which is equivalent to 8.03×10^{-8}?

A −803,000,000

B −0.0000000803

C 0.0000000803

D 803,000,000

Eva chose **D** as the correct answer. How did she get that answer?

_____

_____

_____

_____

Will the solution be a negative number or positive number?

🗨 Pair/Share

Talk about the problem and then write your answer together.

Solve the problems.

1 Which of the following expressions is equivalent to 5,710,900?

A 5.7109×10^{-6}

B 57109×10^2

C 5.7109×10^3

D 5.7109×10^6

2 The average distance from Pluto to the Sun is about 6×10^9 kilometers. The average distance from Mars to the Sun is 2×10^8 kilometers. The average distance from Pluto to the Sun is about how many times as great as the average distance from Mars to the Sun?

⬜ times

3 Last year a business earned 4.1×10^6 dollars in income. This year the business earned 2.05×10^8 dollars in income. Which **best** describes how this year's earnings compare to last year's earnings?

A This year the business earned about 0.5 times as much as it did last year.

B This year the business earned about 2 times as much as it did last year.

C This year the business earned about 50 times as much as it did last year.

D This year the business earned about 100 times as much as it did last year.

4 Write the following numbers in order from *least* to *greatest*.

$$5 \times 10^{-6} \qquad -9 \times 10^{-3}$$

$$-0.0000002 \qquad 0.00007$$

Least ──────────────────────────→ Greatest

5 Cara was using her calculator to solve a problem. The answer that displayed was 1.6E+12. She knows that she entered all of the numbers correctly. Why did the calculator give the answer it did? What is the answer to Cara's problem?

_____

_____

_____

6 The length of a city block running north to south in New York City is about 5×10^{-2} miles. The distance from New York City to Mumbai, India, is about 7.5×10^3 miles. The distance from New York City to Mumbai is about how many times the length of a New York City north-south block?

Show your work.

_____

_____

_____

Answer _____

✓ **Self Check** *Go back and see what you can check off on the Self Check on page 1.*

Lesson 5   Part 1: Introduction

Operations and Scientific Notation

In Lesson 4 you learned to express and compare numbers using scientific notation. Now, take a look at this problem.

> Evaluate the following expression.
>
> $950,000 + (4.6 \times 10^7)$

🔍 Explore It

Use the math you know to answer the question.

- What form is 950,000 written in?_____

- What form is 4.6×10^7 written in? _____

- Write 4.6×10^7 in the same form as 950,000.

  $4.6 \times 10^7 = 4.6 \times$ _____

  $=$ _____

- Write the original addition expression with all numbers in standard form.

  _____

- Explain how you would simplify your expression. What is the sum?

  _____

  _____

  _____

Find Out More

When you add very large (or very small) numbers expressed in standard form, it can be difficult to keep track of all the zeros and make sure the numbers are aligned by place value. One way to deal with these problems is to express each number in scientific notation.

Convert to scientific notation: $950{,}000 = 9.5 \times 100{,}000$
$$= 9.5 \times 10^5$$

Remember that there is a link between place value and powers of 10. Before you can add numbers in standard form, you must align them by place value. Likewise, before you can add numbers in scientific notation, each power of 10 must have the same exponent.

$4.6 \times 10^7 = 4.6 \times (10^2 \times 10^5)$ *Apply the product of powers property.*

$\qquad = (4.6 \times 10^2) \times 10^5$ *Apply the associative property of multiplication.*

$\qquad = 460 \times 10^5$ *Multiply.*

Now that both numbers are expressed with the same exponent, you can find the sum.

$(460 \times 10^5) + (9.5 \times 10^5) = (460 + 9.5) \times 10^5$ *Apply the distributive property.*

$\qquad\qquad\qquad\qquad = 469.5 \times 10^5$ *Add.*

$\qquad\qquad\qquad\qquad = (4.695 \times 10^2) \times 10^5$ *Express in scientific notation.*

$\qquad\qquad\qquad\qquad = 4.695 \times (10^2 \times 10^5)$ *Apply the associative property of multiplication.*

$\qquad\qquad\qquad\qquad = 4.695 \times 10^7$ *Apply the product of powers property.*

Reflect

1 Paul says that $3.14 \times 10^5 + 2.53 \times 10^4 = 5.67 \times 10^5$. Is Paul correct? Explain.

_____

_____

_____

Read the problem below. Then explore how to subtract numbers expressed in scientific notation.

Find the difference: $5.1 \times 10^{12} - 6{,}300{,}000{,}000$

Solve It

Start by converting 6,300,000,000 to scientific notation.

$$6{,}300{,}000{,}000 = 6.3 \times 1{,}000{,}000{,}000$$
$$= 6.3 \times 10^9$$

Picture It

Make a table to help you compare powers of 10.

You cannot subtract numbers expressed in scientific notation unless the powers of 10 have the same exponent. Create a table to help you express the numbers in the problem in scientific notation and compare the exponents.

5.1×10^{12}	6.3×10^9
$= 5.1 \times 10^{12}$	$= 0.0063 \times 10^{12}$
$= 51 \times 10^{11}$	$= 0.063 \times 10^{11}$
$= 510 \times 10^{10}$	$= 0.63 \times 10^{10}$
$= 5{,}100 \times 10^9$	$= 6.3 \times 10^9$

Any pair of numbers from the table with powers of 10 that have the same exponents can be used to solve the problem.

Connect It

Now solve the problem from the previous page.

2 Look at Solve It on the previous page. Write the problem with both numbers expressed in scientific notation.

_____

3 Look at the Picture It on the previous page. Use the table to rewrite the expression you wrote for problem 2. Rewrite that expression so that both terms are written with the same exponent.

_____

4 Use the distributive property to simplify the expression you wrote for problem 3.

_____

_____

5 Write your expression as the product of a decimal times a power of 10.

_____

6 Write your solution in scientific notation.

_____

Try It

Use what you just learned to solve these problems. Show your work.

7 Evaluate: $(7.4 \times 10^{15}) - (9.9 \times 10^{13})$ _____

8 Evaluate: $(8.9 \times 10^5) + (6.5 \times 10^6)$ _____

Read the problem below. Then explore how to multiply numbers expressed in scientific notation.

Multiply: $(5.78 \times 10^5) \times 0.0804$

Estimate It

You can round the factors to estimate the product.

Round 5.78×10^5 to 6×10^5. Then round 0.0804 to 0.08. The estimated product is:
$$(6 \times 10^5) \times (0.08) = 0.48 \times 10^5 = 4.8 \times 10^4$$

You can compare your calculated answer to this estimate to check your solution.

Solve It

You can convert both terms to scientific notation.

Write 0.0804 in scientific notation.

$$0.0804 = \frac{8.04}{100}$$
$$= 8.04 \times \frac{1}{100}$$
$$= 8.04 \times \frac{1}{10^2}$$
$$= 8.04 \times 10^{-2}$$

Write the problem with both factors in scientific notation.
$(5.78 \times 10^5) \times (8.04 \times 10^{-2})$

Connect It

Now solve the problem from the previous page.

9 Complete the equation by applying the associative property to group the decimals and to group the powers of 10.

$(5.78 \times 10^5) \times (8.04 \times 10^{-2}) = $ _____

10 Multiply the decimals and multiply the powers of 10.

_____

_____

11 Apply the properties of exponents to write your solution in scientific notation.

_____

_____

_____

12 Look at Estimate It on the previous page. Is your solution reasonable? Explain.

_____

13 Why is it unnecessary to make the exponents the same before multiplying numbers expressed in scientific notation?

_____

_____

_____

Try It

Use what you just learned to solve these problems. Show your work on a separate sheet of paper.

14 The world's thinnest computer chip is 7.5×10^{-3} millimeters thick. What would be the height of a stack of 3×10^9 chips? _____

15 The speed of a garden snail is about 8.3×10^{-6} miles per second. If a garden snail moves at this speed in a straight line for 3.6×10^3 seconds, how far would the snail travel?

_____

Study the student model below. Then solve problems 16–18.

In this problem you will need to divide numbers expressed in scientific notation.

A hardware factory produces 3.6×10^5 bolts in 2,400 minutes. What is the factory's unit rate of production in bolts per minute?

Look at how you could solve this problem.

$2,400 = 2.4 \times 10^3$ **Express 2,400 in scientific notation.**

$\dfrac{\text{total bolts}}{\text{total minutes}}$ = **unit rate in bolts per minute**

$\dfrac{3.6 \times 10^5}{2.4 \times 10^3} = \dfrac{3.6}{2.4} \times \dfrac{10^5}{10^3}$ **The quotient of products equals the product of quotients.**

$= 1.5 \times 10^{5-3}$ **Subtract the exponents to find the quotient of powers.**

$= 1.5 \times 10^2$

Solution: **The factory produces 1.5×10^2 bolts per minute.**

Pair/Share

Would you rather solve this problem with both numbers expressed in standard form or in scientific notation? Explain.

Which operation will you need to use to solve this problem?

16   A company spends a total of $64,500,000 on salaries for its workers. If the company has 1.5×10^3 workers, what is the average salary per worker?

Show your work.

Pair/Share

Do you need to write each number with the same exponent before you can divide? Explain.

Solution: _____

17 Stalactites are cone-shaped formations that hang from the ceilings of underground caverns. Stalactites can grow at the rate of about 0.005 inch per year. At this rate, what is the length of a stalactite that grows for 7.5×10^4 years?

Show your work.

Would it be easier to solve this problem with numbers in scientific notation, fractions, or as they are written?

Solution: _____

Pair/Share

Compare the stalactite's rate of growth with a child's rate of growth.

18 The volume of the planet Venus is about 928,000,000,000 km³. The volume of the planet Mercury is about 6.08×10^{10} km³. What is the combined volume of Mercury and Venus?

A 9.888×10^{10} km³

B 1.536×10^{11} km³

C 9.888×10^{11} km³

D 1.536×10^{12} km³

Maya chose **D** as the correct answer. How did she get that answer?

_____

_____

_____

_____

How would you express the volume of Venus in scientific notation?

Pair/Share

Talk about the problem and then write your answer together.

Solve the problems.

1 A rancher uses a water bowl for her dog that holds 8,500 milliliters and a water trough for her horse that holds 2.7×10^5 milliliters. How many milliliters of water will the rancher use to completely fill both the bowl and the trough?

A 1.12×10^5 ml

B 2.785×10^5 ml

C 5.8×10^5 ml

D 1.12×10^9 ml

2 The Moon takes about 28 days to orbit the Earth, going a distance of about 2.413×10^6 kilometers. About how many kilometers does the Moon travel during one day of its orbit around the Earth?

A 8.6×10^4 km

B 2.8×10^6 km

C 1.16×10^7 km

D 6.8×10^7 km

3 Jackie incorrectly simplified the following expression.

$(4 \times 10^{-6})(2 \times 10^3) + 1,000$

Select each step that shows an error based solely on the previous step.

A Step 1. $(4 \times 10^{-6})(2 \times 10^3) + 10^3$

B Step 2. $(4 \times 10^{-6})(3 \times 10^3)$

C Step 3. $(4 \times 3)(10^{-6} \times 10^3)$

D Step 4. 12×10^{-3}

E Step 5. 1.2×10^{-4}

4 In October 2009, there were approximately 5×10^7 members of a website. In January 2013, there were approximately 2×10^8 members. How many more members were there in January 2013 than in October 2009? Write your answer in scientific notation. Select from the given digits to complete the sentence.

| 1   2   3   4   5   6   7   8   9 |

There were $\boxed{}.\boxed{} \times 10^{\boxed{}}$ more members in January 2013 than in October 2009.

5 Toshi and Owen need to add 4.9×10^9 and 4.1×10^7. Toshi says they must use the equation $(490 \times 10^7) + (4.1 \times 10^7)$, but Owen says they must use the equation $(4.9 \times 10^9) + (0.041 \times 10^9)$. Are neither, one, or both students correct? Explain.

_____

_____

_____

_____

6 Evaluate $\dfrac{(7.3 \times 10^6) + (2.4 \times 10^7)}{(4 \times 10^4)}$.

Show your work.

Answer _____

✓ **Self Check** *Go back and see what you can check off on the Self Check on page 1.*

Solve the problems.

1 In scientific notation, what is the sum of 2.3×10^{-3} and 5.4×10^{-4}?

  A 2.84×10^{-3}

  B 5.63×10^{-3}

  C 7.7×10^{-7}

  D 12.42×10^{-12}

2 All of the following expressions have a value between 0 and 1, except

  A $\dfrac{(-3^7)}{(-3)^9}$

  B $4^{-10} \times 4^6$

  C $\dfrac{(8^3)^2}{8^{-4}}$

  D $\left(\dfrac{2}{5}\right)^8 \times \left(\dfrac{2}{5}\right)^5$

3 Simplify $(3^3 \times 5^3)^{-2}$.

  A $\dfrac{1}{15^{12}}$

  B $\dfrac{1}{15^6}$

  C 15^{-18}

  D 15^4

4 On a student's scientific calculator, 3×10^5 is displayed as "3 EE 5." In that case, how would the product of 80,000 and 5,000 be displayed on the student's calculator?

The calculator would display the answer as ☐ EE ☐

5 Classify the numbers in the box as perfect squares and perfect cubes. Classify a number by writing it in the appropriate column in the chart. Numbers that are neither perfect squares nor perfect cubes should not be placed in the chart.

| 1 | 27 | 64 | 81 | 100 | 156 | 1,000 | 1,000,000 |

Perfect Squares but NOT Perfect Cubes	Both Perfect Squares AND Perfect Cubes	Perfect Cubes but NOT Perfect Squares

6 The volume of a cube is 343 cubic centimeters. What is the surface area of the cube?

Show your work.

Answer _____

7 The average adult human has approximately 2.5×10^{13} red blood cells and 7×10^9 white blood cells. **About** how many times greater is the number of red blood cells than the number of white blood cells? Write and solve an equation.

Show your work.

Answer _____

Performance Task

Answer the questions and show all your work on separate paper.

The EMCA Toy Company makes a very popular toy for toddlers. It is a set of five stacking cubes that fit inside each other. EMCA needs to redesign this toy so the smallest cube is greater than 3 centimeters tall because it is now too small and a safety risk for toddlers.

Each cube has dimensions that are $\frac{7}{10}$ the height of the next larger cube. One EMCA toy designer thinks the smallest cube should be 5 cm tall. Another toy designer thinks the largest cube should be no more than 15 cm tall. Yet another toy designer would like the middle-sized cube to have the EMCA logo printed on it and thinks this cube should be 10 cm tall.

Make a table showing the relationships among the sizes of each cube. Critique each toy designer's ideas for the dimensions of the cubes. Explain which design you think makes the most sense.

CHECKLIST

Did you . . .

☐ Write and evaluate expressions?

☐ Critique each designer's idea?

☐ Justify your choice for the design?

Reflect on Mathematical Practices

After you complete the task, choose one of the following questions to answer.

1. **Use Structure** Did you use exponents to describe the relationships among the sizes of the different cubes? How did using exponents help?

2. **Critique and Argue** What reasons did you give for your choice of design?

A cookie press is a machine that takes dough in and presses out the cookies to be baked. A juicer is a machine that takes in fruits and vegetables and pours out the juice. A chipper takes in tree branches and blows out wood chips. In mathematics, a machine that takes an input of one number and outputs another number is called a function.

In this unit, you will study linear functions that take an input of one coordinate and output the second coordinate. You will graph coordinates to form a line and examine the properties of the lines you graph.

✓ Self Check

Before starting this unit, check off the skills you know below. As you complete each lesson, see how many more you can check off!

I can:	Before this unit	After this unit
explain what a function is	☐	☐
compare properties of two functions, for example: compare rate of change of a function shown by a graph to the rate of change of a function shown by a table	☐	☐
study the graph of a function and describe it as increasing or decreasing, linear or not linear	☐	☐

Understand Functions

What is a function?

A teacher likes to remind his students that their future earnings are often a function of what they are learning.

What exactly does it mean to say that one thing is a function of another? It relates to dependence. Another way to present the idea above is, "What you are paid depends on what you know."

In mathematics, a **function** is a rule that defines a dependent relationship. A function creates exactly one **output**, or result, for each **input**. The diagram below shows the function "add 2."

| Input = 3 | → | Function: Add 2. | → | Output = 5 |

There is only one possible output for each input.

The function "add 2" is expressed in words. It can also be written as the equation $y = x + 2$, represented in a table of values, and shown as a graph.

🔍 Think   What are some relationships that are functions?

Each coin of American currency is assigned one specific value in dollars. For example, the value of a penny is always $0.01. In this function, an ordered pair relates the name of a coin and its value in dollars.

Coin	Penny	Nickel	Dime	Quarter	Half-Dollar
Dollar Value	0.01	0.05	0.10	0.25	0.50

Most mathematical functions include ordered pairs of numbers. For example, a 120-pound person burns about 65 calories per mile while walking. The table below shows how many calories the person would burn walking different numbers of miles.

Miles (input)	1	2	3	4	5	6
Calories (output)	65	130	195	260	325	390

The input is the number of miles walked. The rule is to multiply the number of miles by 65. The output is the number of calories burned.

🔍 **Think**   What are some relationships that are not functions?

A basketball coach gives the starting players a game jersey. At the same time, he measures the players' heights. This relationship is a function. For each jersey number, he records only one player's height. If jersey number is the input and height is the output, then the relationship is a function.

I see that the height 68 inches is paired with two different jersey numbers.

Player's Jersey Number (input)	10	13	14	18	21
Player's Height in Inches (output)	68	73	75	68	74

Now, reverse the relationship. What if player height is the input and jersey number is the output? The diagram below helps you see that when the input is 68, the output may be either 10 *or* 18. This is not a function. In a function, one input can have only one output.

Input : Height   Output : Jersey Number

68 → 10
73 → 13
74 → 14
75 → 18
     21

✏️ **Reflect**

1 Do the data in this table show a function? If you switch the input and the output values, is it a function? Explain.

Input	3	3	5	5	6
Output	−3	2	4	5	9

<u>I believe that it is a function when you switch the input and output values because every input has exactly one output. According to the data in the table above it can't be a function if the input has two different outputs. but since each input has one number as their output then it is a function!</u>

Explore It

Plot the ordered pairs from each table to represent the relationships as graphs. Then answer the problems.

2 The table below shows the number of dog licenses issued in the town of Palmer over a 5-year period. On the blank graph to the right, label and number the axes. Then plot the ordered pairs.

Year (input)	1	2	3	4	5
Number of Dog Licenses Issued (output)	75	100	125	125	150

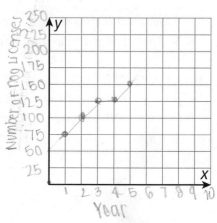

3 Describe the relationship between the input and the output values.

The relationship between the input and the output values is each time the input increases by one the output goes up 25 each time but except for 3 and 4 the output 125 stays the same.

4 Dogs age faster than humans do. Some people claim that dog years are a function of human years, as shown in the table. On the blank graph to the right, label and number the axes. Then plot the ordered pairs.

Age in Human Years (input)	1	2	3	4	5
Age in Dog Years (output)	7	14	21	28	35

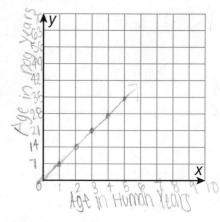

5 Describe the relationship between the input and output values.

The relationship between the input and the output values is that the inputs all increase by one each time, the output goes up by 7 each time. The input multiplied by

💬 Talk About It

Answer the problems below as a group.

6 The relationships on the previous page are shown as graphs. Which graph or graphs show exactly one output for each input? Which set or sets of data represent a function?

The graph that shows exactly one output for each input is the graph that shows age in human years (input) and age in dog years (output) because none of the outputs repeat. each input has one different output. The two sets of data both represent a function because none of the domains repeat and they all have one output value.

7 Think about the function related to dog licenses. Would there ever be one year that is assigned to two different quantities? Explain.

No there would not be one year that it is assigned two quantities because each time it is increasing by twenty-five.

8 Look at your answers to problems 3 and 5 on the previous page. Can you represent either of the functions with an equation? Explain.

The equation for the function for problem 5 is y=7x. The equation is y=7x because each time the input is being multiplied by 7 to get the output value.

✏️ Try It Another Way

Substitute values into the equations to complete the tables. Then state whether the equation represents a function. Explain your reasoning.

9 $y = x + 2$ $y = -2 + 2 = 0$

x (input)	−2	−1	0	1	2
y (output)	0	1	2	3	4

$-1 + 2 = 1$ $1 + 2 = 3$
$0 + 2 =$
$2 + 2 = 4$

10 $y = 4x$

x (input)	−2	−1	0	1	2
y (output)	−8	−4	*Sign & Return*		0

$y = 4(-2) = $ $4(0) = 0$
$y = 4(-1) - 4$ $4(1) = 4$
$4(2)$

The equation does represent a function because when you substitute the values into the equations each input has exactly one different output value.

This equation represents a function because when you plug in the inputs in the equation for x, the inputs all have one output so it is a function. It also represents a function because the rule works each inputs is multiplied by 4 to get the output value.

Connect It

Talk through these problems as a class, then write your answers below.

11 **Arrange:** Use a diagram to represent a function. Put these numbers in the ovals to show ordered pairs that form a function: −4, −3, −3, −1, 1, 2, 5, 5, 6, 7. Complete the diagram that has been started. In the blank diagram, use the same numbers to show a different set of ordered pairs that form a function.

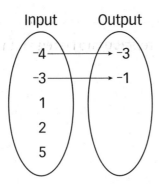
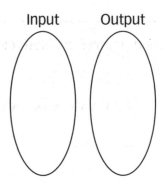

12 **Explain:** A bag includes one number card each for the numbers 1–25. Each of 25 students randomly selects a number card from the bag. Carrie says that if the number is the input and the student's name is the output, the relationship is a function. Mario says that if the student's name is the input and the number is the output, the relationship is a function. Who is correct? Why?

_____

_____

_____

_____

13 **Analyze:** Each molecule of water contains 2 hydrogen atoms and 1 oxygen atom. Complete the table. Is the number of hydrogen atoms a function of the number of oxygen atoms? Explain.

Oxygen Atoms (Input)	1	2	3	4
Hydrogen Atoms (Output)	2			

_____

_____

_____

Put It Together

14 Sean and Rachel were both born on April 17. When Sean was 4, his sister Rachel was 2.

A Write an equation that can be used to determine Rachel's age given Sean's age.
Write an equation that can be used to determine Sean's age given Rachel's age.

_____

_____

B Complete the tables of values to show the relationship between their ages.

Sean's Age (input)	11	12	13	14	15	16
Rachel's Age (output)						

Rachel's Age (input)	1	2	3	4	5	6	7
Sean's Age (output)							

C Describe the relationships in the tables. Is either relationship a function? Explain.

_____

_____

_____

_____

D The problem states that when Sean was 4, Rachel was 2. Sean's age is twice Rachel's age. Can this also be a rule for the relationship between their ages? Why or why not?

_____

_____

_____

_____

_____

You have learned to identify a function. Take a look at this problem.

> Today is a snow day. Felicia decides to track the snowfall. There are already 2 inches of snow on the ground from a previous storm. Felicia measures the snow from today's storm at the end of each hour. She found that exactly 1.5 inches of snow fell each hour. If it snowed at this rate for 5 hours, how much snow was on the ground at the end of each hour?

🔍 Explore It

Use the math you already know to solve the problem.

Time (*h*)	0	1	2	3	4	5
Amount of Snow on the Ground (in.)	2					

- In the table, 0 represents the time before the storm started. How much snow was on the ground then? _____

- How much snow fell in the first hour? _____ So, how much snow was on the ground when Felicia measured at the end of the first hour? Show how you got your answer.

  _____

  _____

- Describe how you can use addition to find the amount of snow on the ground at the end of each hour. Then complete the table.

  _____

  _____

- Suppose you multiply each hour in the table by the rate 1.5 inches per hour. What else do you have to do to find the total amount of snow that is on the ground?

  _____

- Fill in the blanks to write an equation for the situation in the problem. Let *s* equal the amount of snow on the ground and *h* equal the hour. *s* = _____ + _____ • *h*

Find Out More

You are familiar with proportional relationships that start at (0, 0). For example, 0 hours worked means 0 dollars earned. The problem on the previous page does not include (0, 0). The problem states that there were already 2 inches of snow on the ground at 0 hours. This function starts at (0, 2), which is called the **initial value**, or starting value.

Let's look at a graph of this function.

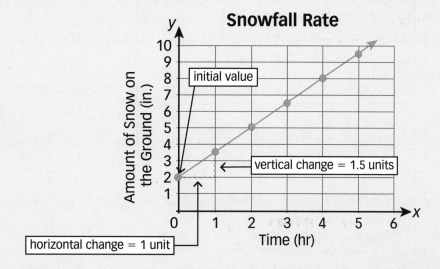

The graph also shows the **rate of change**. The x-values and y-values change at different rates, but the ratio of these values is always the same. From point to point the y-values change by 1.5 units and the x-values change by 1 unit. So, the rate of change is $\frac{1.5}{1}$, or 1.5. You will discover later on in the lesson that functions can have many different initial values and rates of change.

Reflect

1 Dora opened a savings account and deposited $50. When she gets her paycheck each week, Dora will put $25 into the savings account. Describe the initial value and rate of change for this situation.

_____

_____

_____

Read the problem below. Then explore different ways to compare rates of change.

A biologist studied the growth of two different trees over a five-year period. At the beginning of the study, she measured each tree's diameter. The biologist took this same measurement each year to determine the growth.

The red maple in her study had a starting diameter of 4 inches. The diameter grew at an average rate of 0.3 inches per year. The graph on the right shows the growth rate of the silver maple tree. Which function has a greater rate of change?

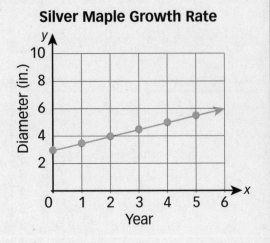

Silver Maple Growth Rate

Graph It

You can use a graph to show the rate of change for the red maple tree.

Make a table of values. At the beginning of the study (year 0) the diameter of the red maple tree is 4 inches. Its diameter grows at a rate of 0.3 inches each year.

Year	0	1	2	3	4	5
Diameter of Tree	4	4.3	4.6	4.9	5.2	5.5

Use the values in the table to make a graph.

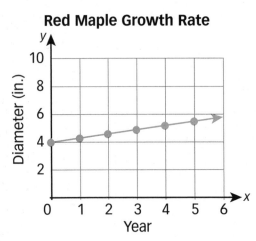

Red Maple Growth Rate

Connect It

Now you can use the graphs to compare the rates of change for both functions.

2 Write ordered pairs for the points that show the initial value on each graph.
Silver Maple: _____ Red Maple: _____
What do the initial values represent in this problem?

_____

3 Fill in the blanks to describe the rate of change for both functions.

On the red maple graph the $\frac{\text{vertical change}}{\text{horizontal change}}$ is $\frac{0.3}{\rule{1cm}{0.4pt}}$.

On the silver maple graph, the $\frac{\text{vertical change}}{\text{horizontal change}}$ is $\frac{\rule{1cm}{0.4pt}}{\rule{1cm}{0.4pt}}$.

4 What do the rates of change represent in the problem?

_____

5 Which function has a greater rate of change? What does that mean in this context?

_____

_____

Try It

Use what you just learned to solve this problem.

6 The table and graph shows how much money a store earns selling each team T-shirt and each team cap. Compare the rates of change for these two functions.

_____

_____

Number of T-shirts Sold	Amount Earned ($)
1	4
2	8
3	12
4	16

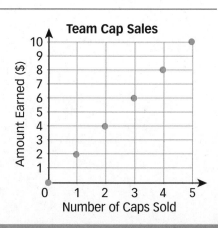

Team Cap Sales

Read the problem below. Then explore different ways to compare functions.

Mrs. White buys a used car for $3,000. She makes monthly payments of $300 until the car is paid for.

Mr. Brown also buys a used car. His monthly payment plan is shown in the table.

Month	0	1	2	3	4	5	6	7	8
Amount Mr. Brown Owes ($)	2,400	2,100	1,800	1,500	1,200	900	600	300	0

Find and compare the rate of change and initial value for each function.

 **Model It**

You can create a table of values for Mrs. White's plan to compare functions.

Her total bill is $3,000, and the monthly payment is $300. The amount owed will continue to decrease by $300.

Month	0	1	2	3	4	5	6	7	8	9	10
Amount Mrs. White Owes ($)	3,000	2,700	2,400	2,100	1,800	1,500	1,200	900	600	300	0

Graph It

You can plot ordered pairs on the same coordinate grid to compare the functions.

As the numbers on the *x*-axis increase, the numbers on the *y*-axis decrease. This shows a negative rate of change.

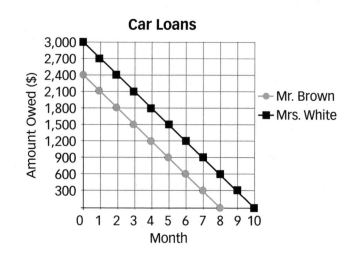

Connect It

Now you can analyze the tables and graphs to compare the functions.

7 Look at the tables on the previous page.

By how much does the amount Mr. Brown owes decrease each month? _____

By how much does the amount Mrs. White owes decrease each month? _____

8 What does your answer to problem 7 tell you about the rates of change for these functions? How does the graph show this?

_____

_____

9 What is the initial value for each function? What do the initial values mean in the context of the problem? _____

_____

10 Fill in the blanks to write an equation for each function, where x = month number and

y = amount owed.   Mrs. White's plan: _____

Mr. Brown's plan: _____

11 Does it take the same time to finish paying for the car with both plans? Explain why or why not by describing the rate of change and initial values.

_____

_____

Try It

Use what you just learned to solve this problem.

12 Below are two companies' rates for textbook rentals. What is the initial value for each function? What is the cost to rent a textbook for 4 months from each company?

Company A: c = $15m$ + 15, where c = total cost and m = number of months

Company B: $19 per month per textbook

_____

_____

Study the model below. Then solve problems 13–15.

The student used the graph to determine Joe's rate. The rates can be used to find the total distance for any time.

Student Model

Justin and Joe are biking downhill. Justin starts 500 feet ahead of Joe and travels at a rate of 44 feet per second. Joe's rate is shown in the graph. After 1 minute, who will be farther down the hill?

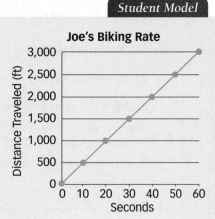

Joe's Biking Rate

Look at how you could show your work.

Possible answer: The graph shows Joe's rate: 50 ft/1 s and

the distance for 60s (1 min) is 3,000 ft. Justin's distance in

1 min = 44 ft/s × 60 s, or 2,640 ft. Add Justin's head start:

2,640 + 500 = 3,140 ft

Solution: Justin will be 140 feet ahead of Joe after 1 minute of

biking.

Pair/Share

Can you solve this problem in a different way?

What do the parts of the equation represent?

13 The equation and table show what two boys pay for gym fees. Compare the rate of change and initial value for each function.

Alfredo

Month	0	1	2	3
Cost	20	30	40	50

Show your work.

Alex

$c = 25 + 10m$, where c = cost and m = number of months.

Pair/Share

How much more will Alex's cost be each month? Why?

Solution: _____

_____

14 Roy wants to buy a new wireless phone for $200. Two stores offer different payment options. Which plan has a greater initial value? Which plan has a greater rate of change?

Store A Payment Plan

Amount Owed ($) vs Week

Store B Payment Plan

Pay $50 at the time of purchase. Pay $20 per month until the phone is paid for.

How does the graph show the initial value?

Show your work.

_____

_____

Solution: _____

_____

Pair/Share

Which option will take longer to pay? How much longer?

15 Which statement about these equations is true?

Equation A: $y = 3x + 4$

Equation B: $y = 5x + 2$

A Equation A has a greater rate of change.

B Equation A has a greater initial value.

C Equation B has a greater initial value.

D Both equations have the same initial value.

Ben chose **C** as the correct answer. How did he get that answer?

_____

_____

_____

How does the graph show the initial value?

Pair/Share

Which option will take longer to pay? How much longer?

Solve the problems.

1 The graph shows a function.

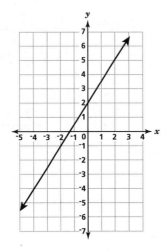

Which equation represents a function with a rate of change that is less than the rate of change of the function shown in the graph? Select all that apply.

A $y = 2x - 4$

B $y = \frac{5}{3}x + 1$

C $y = \frac{3}{2}x - 1$

D $y = x + 3$

E $y = \frac{x}{2} + 5$

2 For each verbal description, write in the correct equation from the choices provided.

Samantha begins her road trip with 30 gallons of gasoline in the tank of her van. Her van gets 25 miles to the gallon. Let *y* represent the number of gallons of gasoline in the tank after *x* miles of travel.		$y = 30 + 0.25x$
		$y = 30 - \frac{x}{25}$
		$y = 25 - \frac{x}{30}$
Evan has a cell phone plan that costs $30 per month and $0.25 per minute of phone use. Let *y* represent the monthly cost of cell phone service after *x* minutes of phone use.		$y = 25 + 0.30x$

3 The rates for two homework help services are shown below.

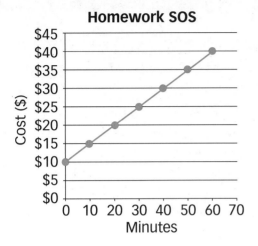

Homework SOS

Homework Lifeline

Rates for Our Services

- Pay $25 to set up an account with our service.

- Then pay $0.40 for each minute of homework assistance that you receive.

Part A

Which service has the greater rate of change? Which has a greater initial value? Describe what this means in the context of the problem.

Show your work.

Answer _____

_____

_____

Part B

What would be the total cost for setting up an account and receiving 90 minutes of homework assistance at each company?

Show your work.

Answer_____

 **Self Check** *Go back and see what you can check off on the Self Check on page 51.*

Lesson 8   Part 1: Introduction

Understand Linear Functions

What do the graphs of different functions look like?

You have worked with functions that have a constant rate of change. You have probably noticed that the graphs of functions with a constant rate of change are straight lines. The lines may start at different points on the *y*-axis, but they continue on a straight path.

What is it about a function that defines its graph as a straight line? Are there functions whose graphs are not straight lines? These are ideas that you will explore in this lesson.

🔍 Think   The graphs of some functions are straight lines.

The formula for the perimeter of a square is $p = 4s$.
The perimeter is 4 times the length of a side.

Side Length (Units)	Perimeter (Units)
0	0
1	4
2	8
3	12
4	16
5	20

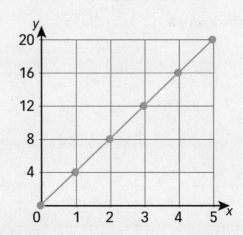

Examine the equation, the table of values, and the graph of this function. You can generalize equations such as $p = 4s$ as $y = mx$. Here is another way to write the equation for this function:

$y = 4x$ └ Rate of Change

The table and the graph show that the rate of change is 4. In the equation $y = mx$, *m* is the rate of change. The *x* and *y* are pairs of values in the ordered pairs shown in the table and graph.

Equations in the form $y = mx$ yield a straight line when graphed. If the graph of a function is a straight line, it is a called a **linear function**. The straight line indicates that there is a constant rate of change between any two points.

Think   The graphs of some functions are not straight lines.

Now let's look at the graph of the area of a square:
$a = s^2$, or $y = x^2$.

+1   +1   +1   +1

Side Length (Units), x	0	1	2	3	4
Area (Square Units), y	0	1	4	9	16

+1   +3   +5   +7

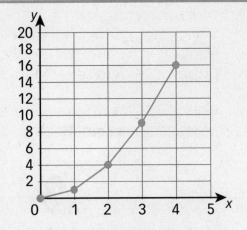

This is not a linear function. It does not have a constant rate of change. Its graph is *not* a line. Let's look at another nonlinear function.

$y = x^2 + 2$

x	y
−3	11
−2	6
−1	3
0	2
1	3
2	6
3	11

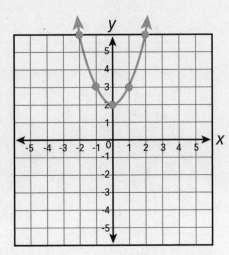

The graph shows that $y = x^2 + 2$ is also not a linear function.

Reflect

1   Give an example of an equation that is a linear function. Explain why it is linear.

An example of an equation that is a linear function is −2x+8 because it has a constant rate of change; it decreases by 2 each time.

Explore It

Graphing is one way to tell whether a function is linear.

2 Consider the equation $y = 2x + 1$. Use the equation to complete the table of values. Then use the table of values to make a graph. Does the equation $y = 2x + 1$ represent a linear function? *Yes it represents a linear function because the line has a 2x+1 rate of change.*

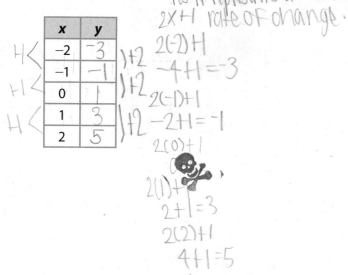

x	y
−2	−3
−1	−1
0	1
1	3
2	5

$2(-2)+1$
$-4+1=-3$

$2(-1)+1$
$-2+1=-1$

$2(0)+1$

$2(1)+$
$2+1=3$

$2(2)+1$
$4+1=5$

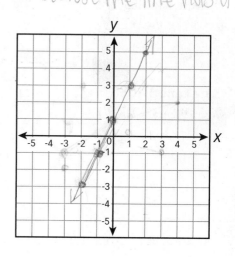

3 Now consider the equation $y = x^3$. Use the equation to complete the table. Then use the values from the table to make a graph. Does the equation $y = x^3$ represent a linear function? *No it doesn't represent a linear function because it has no rate of change.*

$y = x^3$

x	y
−2	8
−1	−1
0	0
1	1
2	8

$y = -2^3$

$y = -1(-1)$
$+1(-1)$
-1

$y = 0(0)(0)$
0

$y = 2 \times 2 \times 2$
$4 \times 2 = 8$

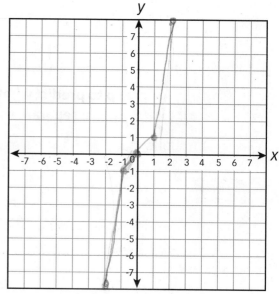

Talk About It

Solve the problems below as a group.

4 Analyze the functions you have seen so far in the lesson. Complete the chart.

Function	$y = 4x$	$y = x^2$	$y = x^2 + 2$	$y = 2x + 1$	$y = x^3$
Initial Value	0	0	2	1	0
Rate of Change	4	varies	varies	2	varies
Equation Form	$y = mx$	$y = mx^2$	$y = mx^2 + b$	$y = mx + b$	$y = mx^3$
Linear or Non-linear?	linear	non-linear	non-linear	linear	non-linear

5 Look at the chart in problem 4. In the equation $y = mx + b$, does m represent the initial value or the rate of change? The m represents the rate of change
What does b represent? The B represents the initial value.
Why? I believe the m represents the rate of change because in the graph it tells you how much to rise and how to run in order to figure out all your points. The b represents the initial value and it is important because it is your y-intercept where the line crosses the y-axis.

6 According to your observations so far, what equation form or forms define a linear function? $y = mx$ and $y = mx + b$ _____ Why do you think this is so?
I believe the two forms are a linear function because they both have a constant rate of change and they both have a slope & y intercept.

✎ **Try It Another Way**

Work with your group to predict whether each equation is a linear function. Then graph each equation on a separate sheet of paper. Describe the results.

7 $y = 0.5x + 2$

_____

_____

_____

_____

8 $y = 0.5x^3$

_____

_____

_____

_____

Connect It

handwritten: y = $40 + 2.50x − y
handwritten: 40

Talk through these problems as a class, then write your answers below.

9 Predict: The cost of a school photo package includes $40 for the photo shoot, plus the number of photos ordered multiplied by the price per photo. Is this situation defined by a linear function? Predict the answer and then write and graph an equation on another sheet of paper to check your prediction. You can use $2.50 or any other value as the cost per photo.

I believe that this situation is a linear function because when you graph them it makes a straight line because it has a constant rate of change.

10 Evaluate: Read two students' answers to a math problem.

Emma: $y = 10 - 2x$ is not a linear function because the graph has a decreasing rate of change.

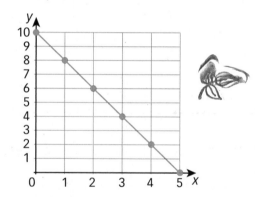

Georgia: $y = 10 - 2x$ is a linear function because it can be written the form $y = mx + b$.

$y = 10 - 2x$

$y = 10 + (-2x)$ Subtracting a positive is the same as adding a negative.

$y = -2x + 10$ commutative property

Who do you agree with? Explain why.

I agree with Georgia that it is a linear function because it goes in a straight line and it has a constant rate of change. I agree with Georgia because it could have a decreasing rate of change it is still a linear function because it has a y-intercept and slope

11 Create: Write an equation that is not a linear function. Justify your answer.

An example of an equation that is not a linear function is y = x⁴ + 10. This is not a linear function because the x can not have an exponent and it doesn't have a constant rate of change.

Put It Together

12 Use what you have learned to complete this task.

> Graph each pair of functions on the same grid using x values of 0, 1, 2, 3, and 4.

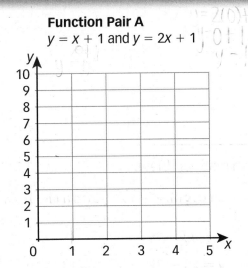

Function Pair A
$y = x + 1$ and $y = 2x + 1$

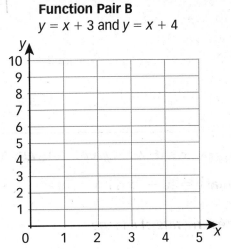

Function Pair B
$y = x + 3$ and $y = x + 4$

A   Answer these questions about Function Pair A.

   i   Are the functions linear or non-linear? _____.

   ii   Do the functions have the same or different rates of change and initial values?

      _____

   iii   How can you describe graphs of other pairs of linear functions with the same
      similarities and differences in the rates of change and initial values?

      _____

      _____

      _____

B   Answer the questions in A.i, A.ii, and A.iii for Function Pair B.

_____

_____

_____

You know how to represent linear functions in different ways. Take a look at this problem.

Wilson Middle School has money left over from last year's fundraiser. This year students are selling discount cards for local businesses. The graph shows the leftover money and the amount the school will earn for each card sold.

Write an equation that shows the total amount of money the school will have, including the leftover money and the amount earned selling x number of cards.

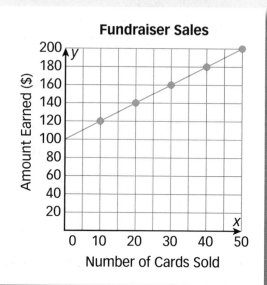

Fundraiser Sales

🔍 Explore It

Use math you already know to solve the problem.

● What does x represent? _____

● What is the rate of change? Explain how you got your answer.

_____

_____

● What does the rate of change represent?

_____

● What is the initial value, and what does it represent?

_____

● Use your answers to write an equation that shows the total amount of money the school will have, including the leftover money and the amount earned selling x number of cards.

$y =$ ____ $x +$ _____

🔍 Find Out More

The rate of change is also known as the **slope** of the graph. Slope is the ratio $\frac{\text{rise}}{\text{run}}$, which tells you how many units the line goes up for every unit that it goes over. In Graph A, the line rises $\frac{1}{2}$ unit for every 1 unit that it goes over. The slope describes the steepness of the line.

Graph A

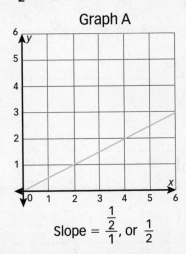

$$\text{Slope} = \frac{\frac{1}{2}}{1}, \text{ or } \frac{1}{2}$$

Graph B

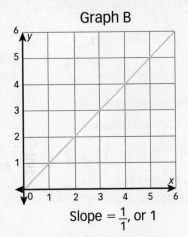

$$\text{Slope} = \frac{1}{1}, \text{ or } 1$$

Graph C

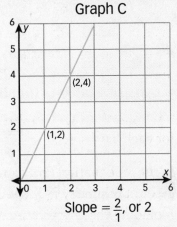

$$\text{Slope} = \frac{2}{1}, \text{ or } 2$$

You can find the slope using any two points on the line.

$$\frac{\text{rise or vertical change}}{\text{run or horizontal change}} = \frac{\text{difference of } y\text{-values}}{\text{difference in } x\text{-values}}, \text{ or } \frac{y_2 - y_1}{x_2 - x_1}$$

Use this formula with two points on Graph C.
Point 1 = (1, 2) and Point 2 = (2, 4).

$$\frac{y_2 - y_1}{x_2 - x_1} = \frac{4 - 2}{2 - 1} \text{ or } \frac{2}{1} = 2$$

The **y-intercept** is the y-coordinate for the point where the graphed line intersects the y-axis. For the graphs above, the y-intercept is 0. The graph on the previous page has a y-intercept of 100.

You can use the slope and y-intercept to write an equation for any linear function. In the equation $y = mx + b$, m is the slope and b is the y-intercept. Because the y-intercepts in the graph above are all 0, the equations are $y = \frac{1}{2}x$, $y = x$, and $y = 2x$.

✏️ Reflect

1 What number will the x-coordinate always be in the ordered pair that identifies the y-intercept? Explain.

_____

_____

Read the problem below. Then explore different ways to find the slope and y-intercept for a linear function.

> Tony's Taxi charges $3 to pick up a passenger, plus $2.50 for each mile. Write an equation for the function that relates the total cost of a trip to the distance. Also identify the slope and y-intercept of the function.

Model It

You can use a table to find the slope and y-intercept.

x	0	1	2	3	4	5
y	3	5.5	8	10.5	13	15.5

When $x = 0$, $y = 3$. The y-intercept is 3. As x increases by 1, y increases by 2.5. The slope is $\frac{2.5}{1}$, or 2.5.

Graph It

You can use a graph to find the slope and y-intercept.

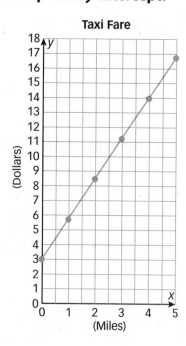

The point on the y-axis is (0, 3), so 3 is the y-intercept. From point to point, the rise is 2.5 and the run is 1. The slope is $\frac{2.5}{1}$, or 2.5.

Connect It

Now you can write an equation for the linear function on the previous page.

2 Explain how you can use a table or graph to find the slope. What does the slope represent in the problem?

_____

_____

_____

3 Explain how you can use a table or graph to find the *y*-intercept. What does the *y*-intercept represent in the problem?

_____

_____

4 In the equation $y = mx + b$, which value represents the slope? _____ Which value represents the y-intercept? _____

5 Use the information from the previous page and above to write an equation for this linear function. _____

6 Check your equation by substituting *x* with one of the *x*-values from the table. Do you get the same *y*-value shown in the table?

_____

Try It

Use what you just learned to solve these problems. Show your work.

7 What is the slope and *y*-intercept of this equation? $y = \frac{3}{4}x + 5$

_____

8 Write an equation for the table of values. Explain how you got your answer.

x	0	1	2	3	4
y	2	5	8	11	14

_____

_____

_____

Read the problem below. Then explore different ways to find the slope and *y*-intercept for a linear function when an equation is given.

A telephone plan charges a regular monthly amount plus charges for the number of minutes of use (*x*) as shown in the equation $y = 0.1x + 40$. What is the slope and *y*-intercept for this function?

 **Model It**

You can use a table to find the slope and *y*-intercept of a function.

Substitute the *x*-values into the equation to find the corresponding *y*-values.

Minutes (*x*)	0	100	200	300	400	500	600
Total Cost (*y*)	40	50	60	70	80	90	100

When $x = 0$, $y = 40$. As *x* increases by 100, *y* increases by 10.

Graph It

You can graph the ordered pairs from a table to show the slope and *y*-intercept of a function.

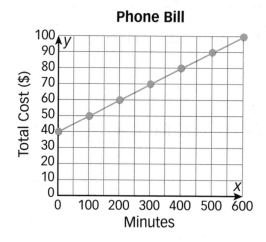

You can use two points on the graph, for example (0, 40) and (100, 50), with the formula $\dfrac{y_2 - y_1}{x_2 - x_1}$ to find the slope.

Connect It

Now you can examine the equation, table, and graph to find the slope and y-intercept.

9 You know that the y-intercept always has an x-coordinate of 0. What number can you substitute for x in the equation to find the y-intercept? Show how to do this.

_____

10 Verify that your answer to problem 9 is correct by describing how the table or graph shows the y-intercept.

_____

_____

11 Explain how to find the slope using the table and graph.

_____

_____

12 Explain how the equation $y = 0.1x + 40$ shows the slope and y-intercept.

_____

_____

13 What do the slope and y-intercept mean in the context of the problem?

_____

_____

14 Describe two different ways to find the slope of a function and two different ways to find the y-intercept of a function.

_____

_____

_____

Try It

Use what you just learned about slope and y-intercepts to solve this problem.

15 A different telephone plan includes a monthly payment of $50 plus a charge of $0.05 per minutes for calls. Write an equation for this function and identify the slope and y-intercept. _____

Read the problem below. Then explore different ways to understand negative slope.

Elena is training for a bike race. She makes this graph to show the relationship between time and distance if she maintains her planned speed. Write an equation for this function. Then identify the slope and y-intercept and explain what each means in the context of the problem.

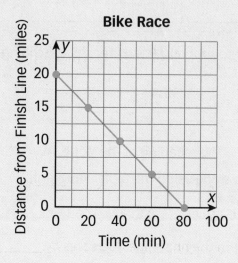

 Model It

You can make a table to find the slope and y-intercept.

x	0	20	40	60	80
y	20	15	10	5	0

The table shows that when $x = 0$, $y = 20$. The y-intercept is 20. As each x-coordinate increases by 20, each y-coordinate decreases by 5. The slope is $-\frac{5}{20}$, or $-\frac{1}{4}$.

 Model It

You can use the information from the graph or table to write an equation.

Use the equation $y = mx + b$. Substitute the slope for m and the y-intercept for b.

$$y = -\frac{1}{4}x + 20$$

Connect It

Now you can relate the slope and *y*-intercept to the information in the problem to interpret their meanings.

16 What do 0 and 20 represent on the *y*-axis of the graph? How long is the race?

_____

_____

17 What do 0 and 80 represent on the *x*-axis? How many minutes will it take Elena to finish

the race? _____

_____

18 Fill in the blanks to show the meaning of the slope. As the time spent racing increases,

the distance from the finish line _____. Every 20 minutes, the distance

from the finish line decreases by _____ miles. The slope, $-\frac{5}{20}$, or _____, means that each

minute, the distance from the finish line decreases by _____ mile.

19 What is the *y*-intercept? _____ What does the *y*-intercept mean in terms of distance from

the finish line? _____

_____

_____

20 Summarize the meaning of the slope and *y*-intercept for the problem on the previous page.

_____

_____

_____

Try It

Use what you just learned about negative slopes to solve this problem.

21 A storm moves at a rate of 8 miles per hour. It is 200 miles away from Freeport and headed directly for this town. The equation $y = 200 - 8x$ can be used to represent this function. Identify the slope and *y*-intercept and explain what they represent.

_____

_____

_____

Study the model below. Then solve problems 22–24.

The student used a table to help write an equation.

Student Model

A lawn mower has a fuel tank that holds 8 gallons of gas. It uses gas at a rate of about 1.25 gallons each hour. Suppose that the gas tank is full. Write an equation that shows how much gas will be in the tank after each hour the lawn mower has run. Identify the slope and *y*-intercept.

Look at how you could show your work in a table.

Hours (*x*)	Gallons of Gas Left (*y*)
0	8
1	6.75
2	5.5
3	4.25
4	3

Start with 8 gallons. Subtract 1.25 gallons each hour.

Solution: $y = 8 - 1.25x$; *y*-intercept = 8 and slope = −1.25

Pair/Share

After how many hours of use will the tank be empty?

How can the labels in the table help you answer this question?

22   Explain what the slope and *y*-intercept represent in the problem above.

Show your work.

_____

_____

Solution: _____

_____

_____

Pair/Share

Is the slope positive or negative? Explain why.

23 Write an equation for the graph. Identify the slope and *y*-intercept.

Show your work.

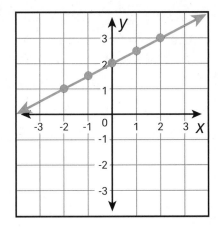

Pair/Share

Write an equation with the same slope but with a *y*-intercept of 4. How would the graph compare with the one shown here?

Solution: _____

24 This equation shows the amount of a candle that is left (in ounces) after burning for *x* hours. What is *y*-intercept for this function, and what does it represent?

$y = 12 - 0.2x$

A   12; the ounces burned each hour

B   12; the ounces in the candle before it burns

C   −0.2; the ounces in the candle before it burns

D   −0.2; the ounces of the candle that burn each hour

Len chose **D** as the correct answer. How did he get that answer?

Pair/Share

How many ounces of the candle would be left after 20 hours?

_____

_____

_____

_____

Solve the problems.

1 Which equation describes the function shown in the table?

x	−2	−1	0	1	2
y	−5	−2	1	4	7

A $y = 2x + 1$

B $y = \frac{1}{3}x + 1$

C $y = 3x + 1$

D $y = 3x$

2 What are the slope and y-intercept of this graph?

A slope = 0.5, y-intercept = 3

B slope = 3, y-intercept = 0.5

C slope = 0.5, y-intercept = 0

D slope = 1, y-intercept = 3

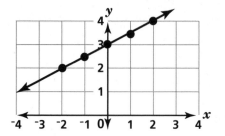

3 A trainer for a soccer team keeps track of the amount of water players consume during practice. The trainer observes that the amount of water consumed is a linear function of the temperature. The graph and equation for this function are shown.

Choose True or False for each statement.

A For every degree increase in temperature, the average amount of water consumed increases by 0.0875 gallons.　□ True　□ False

B When the temperature is below 74 degrees, the average player consumes no water.　□ True　□ False

C When the temperature is 86 degrees, the average player consumes somewhere between 7 gal and 7.2 gal of water.　□ True　□ False

D The amount of water consumed by the average player decreases by 0.45 gallons for every degree the temperature falls.　□ True　□ False

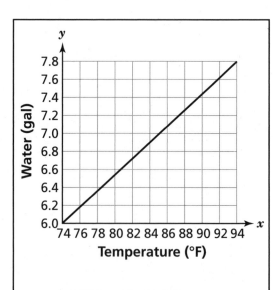

$w = 0.0875t − 0.45$, where w represents the average amount of water consumed, and t represents the temperature on that day.

4 Through which pairs of points is the slope negative? Select all that apply.

A   (3, 6) and (10, 6)

B   (−2, −5) and (0, 0)

C   (1, 9) and (20, 3)

D   (−3, −1) and (3, −3)

E   (16, 11) and (14, 9)

5 A 50-gallon rain barrel is filled to capacity. It drains at a rate of 10 gallons per minute. Write an equation to show how much water is in the barrel after x minutes of draining. Then make a graph for this function.

Show your work.

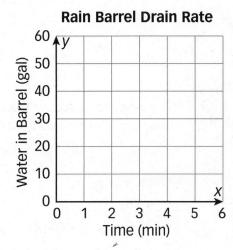

Answer _____

6 Show how to find the slope and y-intercept for the function in problem 5. Explain what each value represents.

Show your work.

_____

_____

Answer _____

_____

_____

 **Self Check**   *Go back and see what you can check off on the Self Check on page 51.*

Lesson 10   Part 1: Introduction 👥

Graphs of Functional Relationships

You know how to interpret slope and *y*-intercept in graphs of linear functions. Take a look at this problem.

Each graph shows distance as a function of time. One graph shows the function when Mr. Dilla is driving in his neighborhood. The other graphs represent Mr. Dilla driving on major city streets and highways. Which description matches each graph below?

Graph A

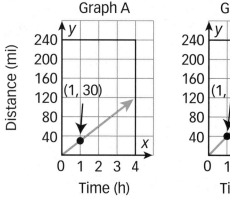

Graph B

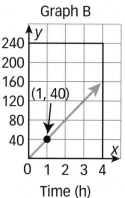

Graph c

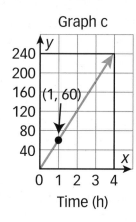

🔍 Explore It

Use math you already know to solve the problem.

▢ What is the slope of each graph? Graph A: _____   Graph B: _____   Graph C: _____

▢ What does the slope mean in each of the graphs? _____

_____

▢ Which graph has the least steep slope? What is the car's speed? _____

▢ Which graph has next steepest slope? What is the car's speed? _____

▢ Which graph has the steepest slope? What is the car's speed? _____

▢ Use this information to match each graph to a type of road in the problem.

_____

_____

_____

🔍 Find Out More

The graph to the right represents Mr. Dilla's drive to work.

This is called a **qualitative graph** because it describes a function visually, not with exact numbers. The sections labeled A, B, and C have the same slope as the graphs with the corresponding letters on the previous page. Qualitative graphs can have sections with horizontal segments. In this case the horizontal segments mean that there is no change or movement. This might mean that Mr. Dilla stopped somewhere along the way.

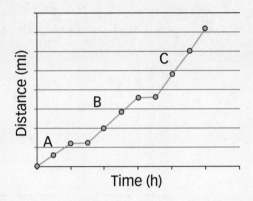

Qualitative graphs can also have curved lines to indicate that the slope, or rate of change, is not constant. The graph to the right shows the number of students who are in the school cafeteria between 11:00 AM and 1:00 PM one school day.

Students go in and out of the cafeteria without following any pattern. The rate is not constant, so this is not a linear situation. The graph shows the following:

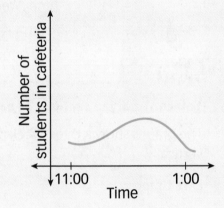

- ▢ The number of students in the cafeteria builds gradually until about 12:00.

- ▢ Between about 12:00 and 1:00 the number of students in the cafeteria decreases gradually.

✎ Reflect

1️⃣ This graph represents a person tossing up a basketball and letting it bounce on the ground. Describe how the graph represents this situation.

_____

_____

_____

_____

Read the problem below. Then explore different ways to help interpret the graph.

Students in Mr. Blanco's class have three weeks to complete their science projects. These graphs show how much of the project two students have completed each day during this three-week period. Describe what each graph shows.

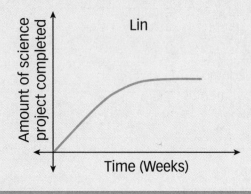

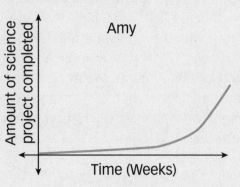

Analyze It

You can analyze sections of each graph.

The graphs show a three-week period. Imagine that the graphs are divided into thirds vertically.

Lin's Graph

- The first third of the graph is steep.

- The second third shows a gradual increase and begins to straighten out.

- The third section is almost a straight horizontal line.

Amy's Graph

- The first and second sections of the graph show a line that is close to being straight.

- The third section is steep.

Solve It

You can use your analysis to write a description of each graph.

Each of the thirds represent one week. Lin's graph is steep in the first third and somewhat flat in the rest. That means she did most of the work on her science project in the first week. Amy's graph is the opposite. The steep section is in the last third. She did most of her work on the project in the third week.

🔍 Connect It

Now you will solve a problem similar to the one on the previous page.

The graph shows daily sales of frozen yogurt at a new store during a six-month period starting on opening day in April. Describe what is happening in terms of this situation for each section of the graph.

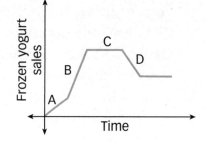

2 Describe and interpret section A.

_____

_____

3 Describe and interpret section B. _____

_____

4 Describe and interpret section C. _____

_____

5 Describe and interpret section D. _____

_____

6 Use your answers to problems 2–5 to summarize what the graph shows.

_____

_____

✏️ Try It

Use what you just learned about qualitative graphs to solve this problem. Show your work on a separate sheet of paper.

7 Summarize the graph showing gasoline prices.

_____

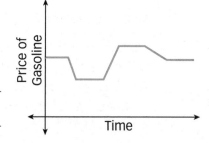

_____

_____

Read the problem below. Then explore different ways to graph the situation.

Angela and Lori are hiking a mountain. The beginning of the trail is not too steep, and they start out at a quick pace. They stop and rest for several minutes then climb a steeper part of the trail at a slower pace until they reach the highest point on the trail. They rest again before climbing down at a constant rate, faster than they climbed the mountain. Sketch a graph to show the distance compared to time.

 **Analyze It**

You can break the story into parts and analyze each part.

A The beginning of the trail is a quick pace. The slope of the segment is steep.

B Before climbing a steeper part they rest. This is a horizontal segment.

C Here the trail is steeper and the pace is slower than section A. The segment is not as steep as part A.

D They rest again, which is another horizontal segment.

E The girls climb down at the quickest pace of the day. This is a steep downward segment. They end up back at the starting point.

 **Graph it**

You can use the analysis to draw a graph.

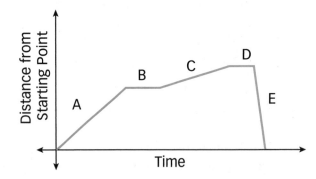

🔍 Connect It

Now you can sketch a graph of a situation similar to the one on the previous page.

Mrs. Elijah does errands on her lunch break. She starts walking quickly, but then has to slow down as the sidewalk gets crowded. She stops at a store and picks up a few items. She walks quickly back to the office since there is no longer a crowd.

8 Describe the first segment of the graph. What should the slope of this segment be like?

_____

9 What should the slope of the graph for this section look like?

_____

10 Describe the third part of the story and tell what the graph looks like for this section.

_____

_____

11 Describe what the graph should look like for the last section. _____

_____

_____

✏️ Try It

Use what you just learned about sketching qualitative graphs to solve these problems.

12 Use the answers to problems 8–11 to sketch a graph for Mrs. Elijah's distance from the office over time. Draw your graph in the space to the right.

13 Pablo starts walking to the park. Halfway to the park he starts jogging. When he gets to the park he stops to rest. Finally, Pablo walks home at the same pace as the first part of his walk. Sketch a graph that shows Pablo's distance from home compared to time. Draw your graph on a separate sheet of paper.

Study the model below. Then solve problems 14–16.

The student analyzes each part of the graph, looking for similarities and differences.

Student Model

This graph shows a child swinging on a swing. Examine the graph and describe what is happening.

Look at how you could show your work by analyzing parts of the graph.

The curves look similar. Each one is a little higher than the one before it.

The bottom of all the curves are on the same horizontal line.

Solution: A swing goes back and forth, reaching the highest point at both ends and the lowest point in the middle of each swing. The graph shows that the child swings a little higher with each swing.

🔁 **Pair/Share**

Why isn't the height of the swing at its lowest point 0?

Which slope is steeper, the one for the bus ride or the one for the walk?

14 Justin takes the bus home from school. He gets off the bus, walks a short distance to his friend's house, and stops to talk. Then he walks to his house. Sketch a graph for this story that compares distance from home to time. Explain your graph.

🔁 **Pair/Share**

How would the graph be different if Justin just walked home without stopping to talk to his friend?

_____

_____

_____

15 This graph shows a carpenter's distance from the ground while working on a house. Describe what could be happening in each section of the graph.

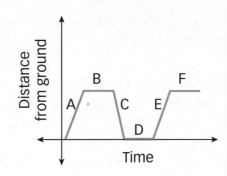

Pair/Share

Think of a similar work story and sketch a graph to represent the situation.

_____

_____

_____

_____

16 This graph shows Mr. Tosti's distance from home as he drives to work one morning. Which section of the graph and corresponding description match?

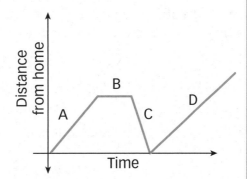

A Section A: Mr. Tosti leaves home, first driving slowly and then picking up speed.

B Section B: Mr. Tosti continues driving at a constant speed.

C Section C: Mr. Tosti forgot something and returned home to get it.

D Section D: Mr. Tosti drives to work, making a stop along the way.

Amir chose **D** as the correct answer. How did he get that answer?

_____

_____

_____

_____

_____

Pair/Share

Does Amir's answer make sense? Discuss.

Solve the problems.

1 Lucy flies from New York to Florida to visit her aunt. The graph shows Lucy's trip from her home in New York to her aunt's house in Florida.

Which part of the graph shows the ride from the airport in Florida to Lucy's aunt's house?

A Section I

B Section III

C Section V

D Section IV

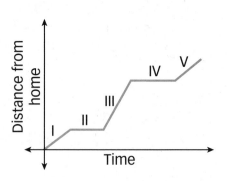

2 The graphs represent parts of Lenny's trip on any given day either from home to school or from school to home. Match the graphs to the descriptions of Lenny's trip shown to the right of the graphs. Next to each graph, enter the number (1, 2, 3, 4) of the description that **best** matches the graph.

A
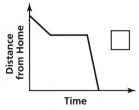

B
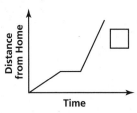

C
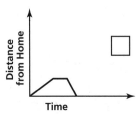

D
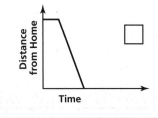

1. Lenny walks to the bus stop, waits for the bus, and then takes the bus to school.
2. Lenny waits for his father to pick him up after school, and his father drives him home.
3. At the end of the school day, Lenny walks to a friend's house and stays there until he takes a bus home.
4. Lenny starts to walk from home to the bus stop. He pauses to check in his book bag for his binder. He realizes he forgot his binder and runs back home to get it.

3 Characterize the behavior of the function within the interval labeled C. Select all that apply.

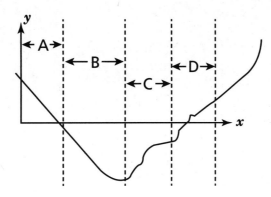

A increasing

B decreasing

C linear

D nonlinear

4 Think about a trip that you have taken, or a route that you travel often. Sketch a graph of the trip or route and write a description.

_____

_____

_____

✓ **Self Check** *Go back and see what you can check off on the Self Check on page 51.*

Solve the problems.

1 Which equation defines a linear function?

A $y = \frac{2}{4}x + 12$

B $y = x^2 + 4x - 6$

C $x^2 + y^2 = 16$

D $\frac{1}{x^2} + \frac{1}{y^2} = 4$

2 Point A is plotted on the coordinate plane below. Determine the location of point D given the following criteria:

• Point D has integer coordinates.

• The graph of line AD is not a function.

Shade in a point that could represent Point D.

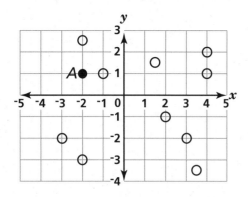

3 Which linear functions below have the same rate of change as one another? Select all that apply.

A

x	y
−2	−21
6	−9
14	3

B $2y - 3x = 1$

C

x	y
−13	−7
−9	−4
−5	−1

D $y = \frac{3}{2}x$

E

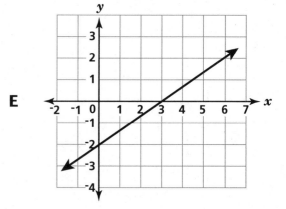

4 Consider the three linear functions below.

x	y
−3	16
0	1
4	−19

$-2x - y = 10$

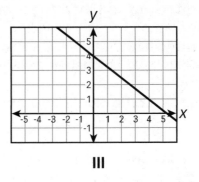

I   II   III

Which linear equation has the greatest rate of change? Explain your answer.

_____

_____

5 While Jenny goes on vacation, she puts her two dogs in a kennel. She pays a flat fee of $20 per dog and then pays a certain amount of money each day for each dog. If she leaves the dogs for 5 days, the cost is $540. If she leaves the dogs for 7 days, the cost is $740.

Part A

Write a linear function to model the relationship between the number of days, x, at the kennel and the total cost, y, for one dog.

Show your work.

Answer _____

Part B

Explain the meaning of the slope in the context of the problem.

_____

_____

Performance Task

Answer the questions and show all your work on separate paper.

Madelyn wants to have her video-themed birthday party at *Fun & More Fun.* She saw this price list on their website:

$300 base price plus $20 per guest for up to 30 guests
31 to 50 guests is an $850 flat fee

Madelyn plans to have 28 guests at her party and would like to figure out how much it is going to cost. After studying the price list, Madelyn suspects something is wrong and is now thinking it makes more sense to invite 31 friends to her party. Use equations and a graph to explain what is wrong with the price list and make a suggestion for how *Fun & More Fun* should fix their pricing plan.

Reflect on Mathematical Practices

After you complete the task, choose one of the following questions to answer.

1. **Use Structure** How did you decide how to represent the different pricing options?

2. **Critique and Argue** How can Madelyn justify her belief that *Fun & More Fun* made a mistake in their pricing?

Many situations can be modeled using a linear function—graphed with a line. When you are comparing two linear functions, you often look for what they have in common. A bakery owner may have one model for the number of cupcakes she can sell in one week at her current price. She may have another model for the number of cupcakes she can afford to make in one week. Examining these two models together will give her the perfect price for her cupcakes. She could use this information to decide how much she can increase the price of cupcakes to make a bigger profit, yet still keep her customers coming back for more.

In this unit, you will solve linear equations and study two linear equations at one time to find a common solution.

✓ Self Check

Before starting this unit, check off the skills you know below. As you complete each lesson, see how many more you can check off!

I can:	Before this unit	After this unit
graph proportional relationships	☐	☐
compare two different proportional relationships	☐	☐
identify the slope of a proportional relationship	☐	☐
graph the line represented by the equation of form $y = mx$ or $y = mx + b$	☐	☐
solve linear equations in one variable, for example: find y if $4(y + 3) = 3(3y - 1)$	☐	☐
give an example of a linear equation that has no solution or many solutions	☐	☐
solve systems of linear equations, for example: find x and y if $y = x - 20$ and $x + y = 84$	☐	☐

Lesson 11   Part 1: Introduction 👥

Represent Proportional Relationships

You know how to identify proportional relationships and linear functions. Take a look at this problem.

Only the top runners in the world can finish a marathon in close to 2 hours. This graph shows the pace that one such runner followed in a race. What is the unit rate?

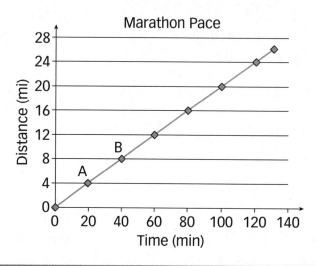

🔍 Explore It

Use math you already know to solve the problem.

◗ Write the coordinates for points A and B. _____

◗ How do you interpret these points in terms of the number of miles run in a given number of minutes? _____

_____

◗ How can you use the information above to find the rate per minute? _____

_____

◗ Find the unit rate. Show your work. _____

◗ What does the unit rate mean in the problem situation? _____

_____

🔍 Find Out More

The unit rate can be represented by the slope of a graph. Compare (0, 0) and (20, 4) in the graph on the previous page. It shows that the rise is 4 and the run is 20. The slope, or $\frac{rise}{run}$ is $\frac{4}{20}$ or $\frac{1}{5}$.

You can also use two points on the graph to find the slope. Use the formula below with (0, 0) and (20, 4). Label one of the coordinates (x_1, y_1) and the other coordinate (x_2, y_2). Then substitute the values for the variables in the formula for the slope.

$$\frac{y_2 - y_1}{x_2 - y_1} = \frac{4 - 0}{20 - 0} \text{ or } \frac{4}{20} = \frac{1}{5}$$

The *y*-intercept of the graph on the previous page is 0. The graphs of all proportional relationships include the point (0, 0), so the *y*-intercept is always 0.

You have seen that equations of linear functions follow the format $y = mx + b$, where *m* is the slope and *b* is the *y*-intercept. The graphs of proportional relationships also fit this format, but the value of *b* is always 0. Let's look at the equation for the graph on the previous page.

$$y = \frac{1}{5}x + 0 \qquad \overset{slope}{\underset{y\text{-intercept}}{}}$$

$$= \frac{1}{5}x$$

This means that all proportional relationships are linear functions in which the *y*-intercept is 0.

✎ Reflect

1. Explain how it is possible that all proportional relationships are linear functions but not all linear functions are proportional relationships.

_____

_____

_____

_____

Read the problem below. Then explore different ways to represent and interpret the unit rate of a proportional relationship.

A website contains hundreds of different recipes. Included with each recipe is a table that gives the approximate cost for different numbers of servings. Find the unit cost for this recipe. Then write an equation for finding the cost of *x* servings.

Roast Chicken with Vegetables and Rice				
Number of Servings	2	4	6	8
Cost ($)	2.50	5.00	7.50	10.00

Picture It

You can use a graph to represent a proportional relationship.

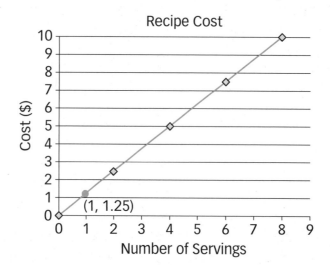

Model It

You can use an equation to represent the unit rate of a proportional relationship.

The graph shows that 1 serving of the recipe costs $1.25.

You can also divide any of the equivalent ratios in the table: $\frac{2.50}{2} = \$1.25$ and $\frac{10}{8} = \$1.25$.

The equation for the cost of *x* servings is the unit rate · number of servings: $y = 1.25x$.

Connect It

Now you will use the table, graph, and equation from the previous page to interpret the unit rate.

2 Describe how the unit rate is shown in the table, graph, and equation.

_____

_____

3 What is the constant of proportionality? How does this relate to the unit rate?

_____

4 What is the slope of the graph? How does this relate to the unit rate and constant of proportionality?

_____

_____

5 Explain what the unit rate means in the context of the problem.

_____

_____

Try It

6 The table shows the function of how many words Gary can read if he reads at a constant rate. Use the information in the table to make a graph, representing the number of minutes on the horizontal axis. Find the slope of the graph and explain what it means in this situation.

Number of Minutes	2	4	6	8
Number of Words	320	640	960	1,280

Read the problem below. Then explore different ways to compare two different proportional relationships.

The table and equation show the rates at which two different printers print in terms of pages per minute. What is the difference between the per page rate of the two printers? Which printer is faster?

Printer A				
Number of Minutes	1	2	3	4
Number of Pages Printed	40	80	120	160

Printer B's printing rate is defined by the equation $y = 50x$, where x is the number of minutes and y is the number of pages printed.

 **Picture It**

You can use the equation for printer B to make a table of values.

Equation: $y = 50x$

Printer B				
Number of Minutes	1	2	3	4
Number of Pages Printed	50	100	150	200

Graph It

You can use the tables to graph the proportional relationships.

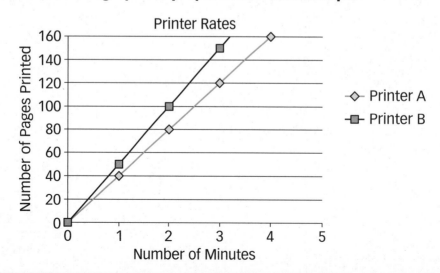

🔍 Connect It

Now you can use the different representations on the previous page to compare the proportional relationships.

7 Explain how to use the tables to find the two unit rates for pages printed per minute.

_____

_____

8 Write an equation that shows the number of pages printed in x minutes for printer A. How do both equations show the unit rates?

_____

9 What are the slopes for each line on the graph?

_____

10 What is the difference between the per page rate of the two printers? Which is faster? Explain how you got the answer.

_____

_____

11 How can you compare unit rates when proportional relationships are represented in different ways? For example, if one relationship is represented by a table and another by a graph?

_____

_____

✏️ Try It

12 The price for x pounds of almonds at the Snack Shack is represented by $y = 6.5x$ and the cost at the Nut Hut is shown in the graph. Which store sells almonds at a lower unit cost? How much lower?

_____

_____

_____

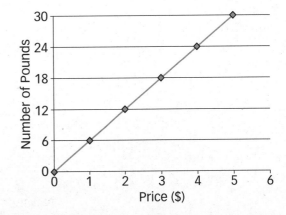

Study the model below. Then solve problems 13–15.

The student used the graph to find the unit rate and then compared unit rates.

Student Model

Corey researched some animal speed records. He found that a horse ran at a rate of 16.5 meters per second. A jackrabbit's rate is shown in the graph. Which animal ran at a faster rate? How much faster per second?

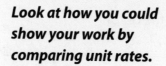

Jackrabbit Speed

Look at how you could show your work by comparing unit rates.

horse's rate: 16.5 $\frac{m}{s}$

jackrabbit's rate: 30 m in 2 s, or 15 $\frac{m}{s}$

16.5 − 15 = 1.5

Solution: _The horse ran 1.5 $\frac{m}{s}$ faster than the jackrabbit._

 Pair/Share

Express each rate as kilometers per hour.

It may be helpful to look at points that fall directly on horizontal lines in the graph.

13 What is the slope of the graph?

Show your work.

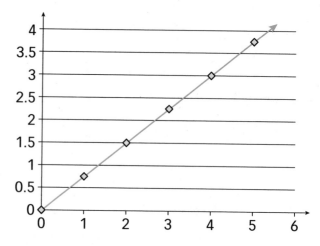

 **Pair/Share**

What are some other names for slope?

Solution: _____

14 The equation $u = 0.99c$ shows the value of the U.S. dollar compared to the Canadian dollar on one particular day, where c = the value of the Canadian dollar and u = the value of the U.S. dollar. The table shows the value of the U.S. dollar compared to the Australian dollar on the same day. Was the U.S. dollar closer in value to the Canadian dollar or the Australian dollar that day?

Australian Dollar	1	2	3	4
U.S. Dollar	0.95	1.90	2.85	3.80

Show your work.

Solution: _____

_____

15 The unit cost per pound for green beans is represented by the equation $y = 1.2x$. Which of these points is NOT on the graph of this proportional relationship?

A (0, 0)

B (2, 2.4)

C (4, 4.8)

D (12, 10)

Al chose **A** as the correct answer. How did he get that answer?

_____

_____

_____

Make sure you compare the dollars in the same order.

Pair/Share

If you have ten U.S. dollars, how much is it worth in Canadian dollars? in Australian dollars?

Can you solve this problem without making a graph?

Pair/Share

What are some other points on this graph?

Solve the problems.

1 Find the equation for the unit cost of the pens.

Number of Pens (*p*)	5	10	15	20
Cost (*c*)	$3.95	$7.90	$11.85	$15.80

A $c = 1.27p$ **C** $c = 3.95p$

B $c = 0.79p$ **D** $c = 5p$

2 Which of the following is the fastest unit rate? (1 mile = 1,760 yards = 5,280 feet)

A 30 miles per hour   **C** 700 yards per minute

B 40 feet per second   **D** 2,200 feet per minute

3 Look at the three graphs below.

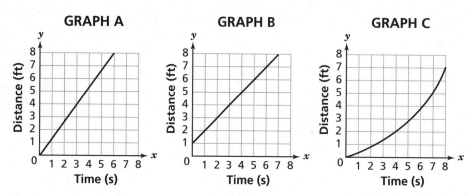

Based on the graphs, choose True or False for each statement.

A Graph B shows a proportional relationship between distance and time. ☐ True ☐ False

B In Graph A, the constant of proportionality between distance and time is $\frac{4}{3}$. ☐ True ☐ False

C Graph C shows an object that speeds up over time. ☐ True ☐ False

D The unit rate in Graph B is 2 feet per second. ☐ True ☐ False

E An object represented by Graph A is moving faster than an object represented by Graph B. ☐ True ☐ False

4   A grocery store sells Brand A olive oil in a 33-ounce bottle for $16.50. The store also sells a
Brand B olive oil in a large dispenser that customers can buy for $4.80 per cup. Graph each
proportional relationship on the same graph. Identify the unit cost for each and tell which is
the better buy.

1 cup = 8 fluid ounces

Show your work.

Answer _____

_____

5   A craft store buys 50 yards of satin ribbon for $13.50. The store sells the ribbon by the foot. A
customer can purchase 5 feet of ribbon for $0.80. How much profit does the craft store earn if
it sells 45 yards of the ribbon and scraps the rest?

Show your work.

Answer _____

 **Self Check**   *Go back and see what you can check off on the Self Check on page 99.*

Understand the Slope-Intercept Equation for a Line

How can you show that an equation in the form $y = mx + b$ defines a line?

You have discovered in previous lessons that linear equations follow the format $y = mx + b$. These equations are written in **slope-intercept form**, because you can identify the slope (m) and y-coordinate of the y-intercept (b) from the equation. If the y-coordinate of the y-intercept (b) is 0, then the equation simplifies to $y = mx$. Now you will see why linear equations can be written this way by examining slopes and similar triangles.

🔍 **Think**   How does slope relate to triangles?

To understand slope, it helps to understand similar triangles. **Similar triangles** are scale drawings of one another—they have the same shape but can have a different size. The corresponding sides of similar triangles are proportional, and the corresponding angles have equal measures. Triangles *ABC* and *DEF* are similar triangles.

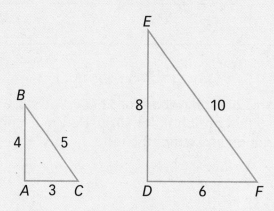

$$m\angle A = m\angle D \qquad\qquad m\angle B = m\angle E \qquad\qquad m\angle C = m\angle F$$

$$\frac{AB}{DE} = \frac{4}{8}, \text{ or } \frac{1}{2} \qquad\qquad \frac{BC}{EF} = \frac{5}{10}, \text{ or } \frac{1}{2} \qquad\qquad \frac{AC}{DF} = \frac{3}{6}, \text{ or } \frac{1}{2}$$

Each side of triangle *ABC* is half the length of the corresponding side of triangle *DEF*. Each side of triangle *DEF* is twice the length of the corresponding side of triangle *ABC*.

🔍 **Think** A coordinate grid can be used to compare similar triangles.

You can examine the corresponding sides and angles of similar triangles drawn along a non-vertical line on a coordinate grid.

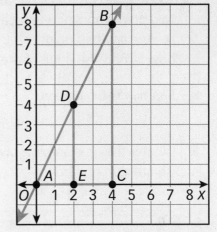

Both triangles ABC and ADE contain $\angle A$, and $m\angle A = m\angle A$. Because $\angle C$ and $\angle E$ are both right angles, their measures are also equal. The sum of the angle measures of all triangles is $180°$. So the measures of $\angle B$ and $\angle D$ must also be equal.

Since all three corresponding angles have the same measure, the triangles are similar. That means that the sides are proportional: $\dfrac{DE}{BC} = \dfrac{AE}{AC}$. The $\dfrac{\text{rise}}{\text{run}}$ is also proportional: $\dfrac{DE}{AE} = \dfrac{BC}{AC}$.

You could draw other triangles like these along the line. The $\dfrac{\text{rise}}{\text{run}}$ ratio will always be equal and the triangles will always be similar.

🔍 **Think** You can calculate the slope (m) of a line using any two points on the line.

Use the formula $m = \dfrac{y_2 - y_1}{x_2 - x_1}$ with different pairs of points.

A (0, 0) and D (2, 4): $\dfrac{4 - 0}{2 - 0} = \dfrac{4}{2}$, or 2

D (2, 4) and B (4, 8): $\dfrac{8 - 4}{4 - 2} = \dfrac{4}{2}$, or 2

A (0, 0) and B (4, 8): $\dfrac{8 - 0}{4 - 0} = \dfrac{8}{4}$, or 2

✏️ **Reflect**

1 What do the similar triangles tell you about the slope of a line segment between any two non-vertical points?

_____

_____

_____

Explore It

Follow the directions to solve the equation. Fill in the blanks as you go.

2 You learned on the previous page that the slope between any two points on a non-vertical line is the same. Let m = slope and (x, y) = any two points on the line. Fill in the blanks to show how to find the slope of the line using $(0, 0)$ and (x, y).

2. $m = \dfrac{y - \boxed{}}{\boxed{} - 0}$

3 Simplify the equation.

3. $m = \dfrac{\boxed{}}{\boxed{}}$

4 What is the next step in solving the equation if you want to isolate y on one side?

4. $m \cdot \boxed{} = \dfrac{\boxed{} \cdot \boxed{}}{\boxed{}}$

_____

5 Simplify.

5. $\boxed{} = \boxed{}$

6 Rewrite the equation with y on the left side.

6. $\boxed{} = \boxed{}$

7 How do you know that the graph on the previous page represents a proportional relationship?

_____

8 Explain the reasoning used in problems 2–6 to find a general equation for all proportional relationships.

_____

_____

_____

_____

_____

_____

💬 Talk About It

Solve the problems below as a group.

9 What is the slope of the line in this diagram? _____
   What is the y-intercept? _____

10 Compare the slope and y-intercept of this diagram
   with the one in the introduction. How are they similar?
   How are they different?

   _____

   _____

   _____

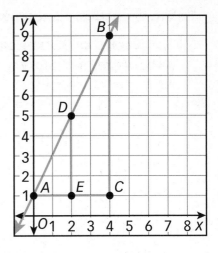

11 Write the coordinates for each labeled point in the diagram.

   _____

12 Compare these coordinates to the ones in the diagram in the introduction. What do you
   notice? How does this affect the position of the line and triangles on the grid?

   _____

   _____

   _____

   _____

13 How do you know that the graph on this page represents a linear function that is not a
   proportional relationship?

   _____

   _____

✏️ Try It Another Way

14 Use the y-intercept (0, b) and any other point on the line (x, y) to derive the general form
   of a linear equation $y = mx + b$. Look at the steps in Explore It to guide you.

   _____

15 How is your equation in problem 14 different from $y = mx$? What does this mean?

   _____

   _____

🔍 Connect It

Talk through these problems as a class, then write your answers below.

16 Compare: Look at these equations. Do you think they are all linear equations? Can they all be written in the form $y = mx + b$? If so, show how.

$$y = 2x - 3 \qquad y - 2 = x + 2 \qquad 3x = 9 + 3y$$

17 Analyze: Alana used the table of values to find the slope of the graph for this function. Analyze her work and explain why you do or don't agree with her.

x	2	4	6	8
y	4	5	6	7

$$m = \frac{6 - 2}{6 - 4} = \frac{4}{2}, \text{ or } 2$$

18 Verify: Explain how to find the slope and y-intercept by just looking at the equation $y = \frac{1}{3}x - 2$. Then graph the equation and verify your answers.

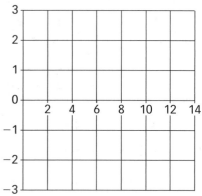

Put It Together

19 Use what you have learned to complete this task.

A Show how to find the slope of a line that passes through the points in the table.

x	−3	0	3	6
y	5	1	−3	−7

_____

_____

B Graph the data in the table. Using the graph, show how to find the slope in a different way than you did in part A.

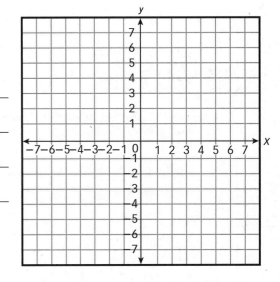

_____

_____

_____

C Show how to write an equation for the table and graph. Verify that the equation works with the table and the graph.

_____

_____

_____

_____

Lesson 13   Part 1: Introduction

Solve Linear Equations with Rational Coefficients

CCSS
8.EE.C.7b

You've learned how to solve linear equations with variables on one side of the equation. In this lesson, you'll learn how to solve linear equations with variables on both sides of the equation. Take a look at this problem.

The square and equilateral triangle shown have the same perimeter. What is the value of x?

$x + 3$ $\qquad$ $3x - 1$

Explore It

Use the math you already know to solve this problem.

◼ The perimeter of the square is $4(x + 3)$, and the perimeter of the triangle is $3(3x - 1)$. Because the perimeters are the same, $4(x + 3) = 3(3x - 1)$. Try substituting 3 for x in the equation. Do you get a true statement? Explain.

_____

_____

_____

_____

◼ Use the distributive property to transform $4(x + 3) = 3(3x - 1)$ into a simpler form without parentheses. _____

◼ Substitute 3 for x in your new equation. Do you get a true statement? Explain.

_____

_____

_____

◼ You can transform $4x + 12 = 9x - 3$ again into a simpler form by subtracting $4x$ from both sides to get $12 = 5x - 3$. If you substitute 3 for x in $12 = 5x - 3$, do you still get a true statement? _____

◼ You can continue to transform $12 = 5x - 3$ into a simpler form by adding 3 to both sides to get $15 = 5x$. When $x = 3$, do you get a true statement? _____

◼ Finally, divide both sides of $15 = 5x$ by 5. What is the result? _____

Find Out More

In Explore It, you transformed the original equation into simpler and simpler forms. Each time, substituting 3 for x resulted in a true statement. The transformations don't change the solution to the equation.

You transform equations to get to the form $x = a$ because that gives you the solution to the equation you started with. You can add and subtract variables from both sides of the equation just as you do with constants.

Look at a step-by-step solution of $4(x + 3) = 3(3x - 1)$.

$$4(x + 3) = 3(3x - 1)$$
$$4x + 12 = 9x - 3 \qquad \text{Apply the distributive property.}$$
$$\underline{-4x \qquad\qquad -4x} \qquad \text{Subtract } 4x \text{ from both sides so that the}$$
$$12 = 5x - 3 \qquad \text{variable occurs on just one side.}$$
$$\underline{+3 \qquad\qquad +3} \qquad \text{Add 3 to both sides.}$$
$$\frac{15}{5} = \frac{5x}{5} \qquad \text{Divide both sides by 5.}$$
$$3 = x$$

There is often more than one way to solve an equation.

$$4(x + 3) = 3(3x - 1)$$
$$4x + 12 = 9x - 3 \qquad \text{Apply the distributive property.}$$
$$\underline{-9x \qquad\qquad -9x} \qquad \text{Subtract } 9x \text{ from both sides so that the}$$
$$-5x + 12 = -3 \qquad \text{variable occurs on just one side.}$$
$$\underline{-12 \qquad -12} \qquad \text{Subtract 12 from both sides.}$$
$$\frac{-5x}{-5} = \frac{-15}{-5} \qquad \text{Divide both sides by } -5.$$
$$x = 3$$

Reflect

1 How do you solve multi-step equations that have variables on both sides?

_____

_____

_____

Read the problem below. Then explore different ways to solve an equation.

On a math quiz, Elise and Kaitlyn solved the equation $\frac{1}{2}(5x - 6) = 3x$ in different ways, but each student arrived at the correct answer. Describe the steps that each student took to solve the equation. An explanation of the first step for each method has been provided.

Solve It

Elise solved the problem in this way.

$$\frac{1}{2}(5x - 6) = 3x$$

$$\frac{5}{2}x - 3 = 3x \qquad \textbf{Step 1} \text{ Apply the distributive property.}$$

$$\underline{-\frac{5}{2}x \qquad\quad -\frac{5}{2}x} \qquad \textbf{Step 2} \text{ Subtract } \frac{5}{2}x \text{ from each side.}$$

$$\frac{-3}{\frac{1}{2}} = \frac{\frac{1}{2}x}{\frac{1}{2}} \qquad \textbf{Step 3} \text{ Divide both sides by } \frac{1}{2}.$$

$$-6 = x$$

Solve It

Kaitlyn solved the problem in this way.

$$\frac{1}{2}(5x - 6) = 3x$$

$$2 \cdot \frac{1}{2}(5x - 6) = 2 \cdot 3x \qquad \textbf{Step 1} \text{ Multiply both sides by 2.}$$

$$5x - 6 = 6x$$

$$\underline{-5x \qquad\quad -5x} \qquad \textbf{Step 2} \text{ Subtract 5x from both sides.}$$

$$-6 = x$$

💡 Connect It

Now you will analyze how each student solved the equation.

2 Look at Elise's solution method. She took three steps to solve the equation. Describe

Step 2. _In Step 2 Elise did the additive inverse of 5x because she wants to cancel it out so she can get 5x on the other side of the equation._

Why do you think Elise took that step? _I think this took this step because she wanted to have the variable by itself so she had to make it cancel out._

3 Describe Step 3 in Elise's solution. _For step 3 Elise divided both sides by ⅓ because she wants to get the x by itself so she can find the value of x._

Could Elise have used a different step? Explain. _She could have just multiplied both sides_

of the equation by 2 instead of dividing both sides of ½.

4 Look at Kaitlyn's solution method. Describe Step 2 in her solution. _In Step 2 Kaitlyn did the_

additive inverse of 5x so she could get the variable by itself.

Why do you think she took that step? _She took this step because she wanted to find the value for x so she got the variable by itself._

5 Which method do you prefer? Explain your thinking. _I prefer to use Kaitlyn's method because_

you could just multiply both sides by 2 instead of doing distributive property which you have

on improper fraction so it much easier if you multiply by 2.

6 Explain how to check the solution to an equation. Then show how to check the solution to the equation on the previous page. _You check the solution to an equation by plugging_

in the value you get from the variable. Then you solve the equation and

see if you get the same answer as your first equation.

✏️ Try It

Use what you learned about different ways to solve linear equations. Show your work.

7 Solve the equation and check your solution: $10 = \frac{1}{3}(x - 15)$.

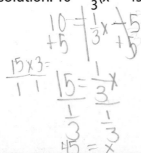

$$10 = \frac{1}{3}x - 5$$
$$+5 \qquad +5$$
$$15 \times 3 = \qquad 15 = \frac{1}{3}x$$
$$\frac{}{11} \qquad \frac{1}{3} \qquad \frac{1}{3}$$
$$45 = x$$

$$10 = \frac{1}{3}(45-15)$$
$$\frac{1}{3}(30)$$
$$\frac{1 \cdot 30}{3 \cdot 1} = \frac{30 \div 3}{3 \div 3} = \frac{10}{1}$$
$$10 = 10 \checkmark$$

Study the student model below. Then solve problems 8–10.

The student multiplied each side of the equation by 10 to transform the equation into one without decimals.

Student Model

Solve the following equation for r.

$$16.5 + 1.5r = 12 + 2r$$

Look at how you can show your work.

$$16.5 + 1.5r = 12 + 2r$$
$$10(16.5 + 1.5r) = 10(12 + 2r)$$
$$165 + 15r = 120 + 20r$$
$$\underline{ - 15r \qquad\qquad - 15r}$$
$$165 = 120 + 5r$$
$$\underline{-120 \quad\; -120}$$
$$\frac{45}{5} = \frac{5r}{5}$$

Solution: $\underline{\quad 9 = r \qquad\qquad\qquad\qquad\qquad\qquad\qquad}$

Pair/Share

Can you solve this equation in another way?

What equation can you write to solve the problem?

8 One fifth of a number plus three times the number is equal to twice the number plus 42. What is the number?

Show your work.

Pair/Share

How can you check your answer?

Solution: _____

9 Show two different ways to solve $\frac{1}{4}x - 5 = \frac{3}{4}x - 12$.

Show your work.

Can you multiply both sides of the equation by a number to get a simpler equation without fractions?

Solution: _____

Pair/Share

Justify the steps you took to solve the equation.

10 Which equation has the same solution as $\frac{1}{2}(6 - x) + 3x = \frac{1}{2}x - 8$?
Circle the letter of the correct answer.

A $3 + 2x = \frac{1}{2}x - 8$

B $6 - x + 3x = x - 16$

C $3 + \frac{5}{2}x = \frac{1}{2}x - 8$

D $6 - x + 3x = x - 8$

Haley chose **A** as the correct answer. How did she get that answer?

_____

_____

_____

_____

_____

What properties and operations can you use to simplify both sides of an equation?

Pair/Share

How would you help Haley understand her error?

Solve the problems.

1 Find the solution of $5 + 3(y - 4) = 5(y + 2) - y$.

A $10\frac{1}{2}$ **C** -1

B $7\frac{1}{3}$ **D** -17

2 Which equation does NOT have the same solution as $\frac{1}{3}(9 - 2x) = x + 1$?

A $2 = 1\frac{2}{3}x$ **C** $9 - 2x = 3x + 3$

B $3 - 2x = x + 1$ **D** $-5x = -6$

3 Three students solved the equation $2(3x - 8) = 32$ in different ways, but each student arrived at the correct answer. Select all of the solutions that show a correct method for solving the equation.

A $\frac{1}{2} \cdot 2(3x - 8) = 32 \cdot \frac{1}{2}$ **B** $2(3x - 8) = 32$ **C** $2(3x - 8) = 32$

           $3x - 8 = 16$ $5x - 8 = 32$ $\frac{6x}{6} - \frac{16}{6} = \frac{32}{6}$

              $3x = 24$ $5x = 40$ $x = \frac{48}{6}$

                 $x = 8$ $x = 8$ $x = 8$

4 Consider the equation $2(4x - 5) = ax + b$. From the list of digits provided, determine the values of a and b that make the solution to this equation $x = 3$.

$$\boxed{0 \quad 1 \quad 2 \quad 3 \quad 4}$$

$a = \boxed{}$ $b = \boxed{}$

5 Solve the equation $x + 0.7 = 1 - 0.2x$ in two different ways. Then check your answer.

Show your work.

6 A square and an equilateral triangle have the same perimeter. Each side of the triangle is 4 inches longer than each side of the square. What is the perimeter of the square?

Show your work.

Answer The perimeter of the square is _____ inches.

 **Self Check** *Go back and see what you can check off on the Self Check on page 99.*

Lesson 14   Part 1: Introduction 👥

Solutions of Linear Equations

CCSS
8.EE.C.7a

You've learned how to solve linear equations and how to check your solution. In this lesson, you'll learn that not every linear equation has just one solution. Take a look at this problem.

> Jason and his friend Amy are arguing. Jason says that a linear equation always has just one solution. Amy says that some linear equations have more than one solution. Who's right? Amy asked Jason to explore solutions to the following equation.
>
> $$2x + 1 + x = 3(x - 2) + 7$$

🔍 Explore It

Use the math you already know to solve this problem.

Remember that a solution to an equation is a number that makes the equation true. To check to see if a number is a solution to this equation, replace *x* with its value.

- Is 6 a solution to the equation? Show your work. _____

- Is −2 a solution to the equation? Show your work. _____

- Is 0 a solution to the equation? Show your work. _____

- Can an equation have more than one solution? Explain. Who is right—Jason or Amy?

_____

Find Out More

Look at how you could solve Amy's equation.

$$2x + 1 + x = 3(x - 2) + 7$$

First, simplify each side:

Use the distributive property. $\quad 2x + 1 + x = 3x - 6 + 7$

Combine like terms. $\qquad\qquad 3x + 1 = 3x + 1$

Once both sides of an equation are in simplest form, you can say a lot about the solution without actually solving the equation. You can just look at the structure.

Think about how you might solve this equation with pictures. Look at the pan balance below. The left pan represents $3x + 1$. So does the right pan.

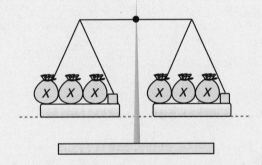

If you take away $3x$ from both sides, you end up with $1 = 1$, a true statement. If you take away 1 from both sides, you end up with $3x = 3x$, a true statement. You can replace x with any number and you will always get a true statement. The pan will remain balanced. This equation has infinitely many solutions.

You've seen that a linear equation can have one solution or, in a case like this, infinitely many solutions. You will also see that a linear equation can have no solution.

Reflect

1 Once both sides of an equation are in simplest form, how can you tell if it has infinitely many solutions?

_____

_____

_____

Read the problem below. Then explore how to identify when an equation has one solution, infinitely many solutions, or no solution.

Yari and her friends, Alyssa and David, were each given an equation to solve.

Yari: $2(x + 10) - 17 = 5 + 2x - 2$

Alyssa: $5x + 3 - 3x = 2(x + 3) - 5$

David: $2(x - 3) + 9 = 5 + x - 1$

Whose equation has one solution? Infinitely many solutions? No solution?

🔍 Model It

You can use properties of operations to simplify each side of Yari's equation.

$2(x + 10) - 17 = 5 + 2x - 2$

$2x + 20 - 17 = 3 + 2x$

$2x + 3 = 3 + 2x$

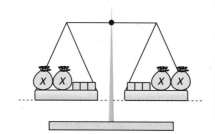

The variable terms and the constants are the same on both sides of the equation. No matter what value you choose for x, the equation will always be true.

🔍 Model It

You can use properties of operations to simplify each side of Alyssa's equation.

$5x + 3 - 3x = 2(x + 3) - 5$

$2x + 3 = 2x + 6 - 5$

$2x + 3 = 2x + 1$

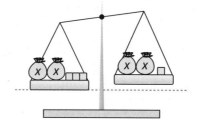

The variable terms are the same on both sides of the equation but the constants are different. There is no value for x that will make the equation true.

🔍 Model It

You can use properties of operations to simplify each side of David's equation.

$2(x - 3) + 9 = 5 + x - 1$

$2x - 6 + 9 = 4 + x$

$2x + 3 = 4 + x$

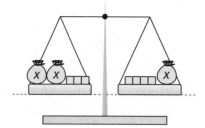

The variable terms are different. There is only one value for x that will make the equation true.

Connect It

Now you will use the models to solve this problem.

2 Look at Model It for Yari's equation. What do you notice about both sides of the equation? What equation do you get if you subtract 2x from both sides of the equation?

_____

3 Look at Model It for Alyssa's equation. How is it different than Yari's equation? How is it similar?

_____

_____

_____

4 Look at the pan balance for Alyssa's equation. Is there any way to balance the pan? Explain. What equation do you get if you subtract 2x from both sides of the equation?

_____

_____

5 Look at the Model It for David's equation. Are the variable terms on each side of the equation the same or different? _____ Solve David's equation. _____

6 Explain how you know when an equation has one solution, no solution, or infinitely many solutions.

_____

_____

_____

_____

Try It

Use what you just learned about equations with one solution, no solution, or infinitely many solutions. Show your work on a separate sheet of paper.

Replace c and d in the equation $cx + d = 8x + 12$ with the given values. Explain why the equation has one solution, no solution, or infinitely many solutions.

7 $c = 6$ and $d = 34$ _____ **8** $c = 8$ and $d = 6$ _____

Study the student model below. Then solve problems 9–11.

Student Model

> The student solved the equation to find that 0 is a solution.

Michelle looks at the equation $-6x - 30 = 6x - 30$ and says there is no solution. Is she correct? Explain.

Look at how you can show your work.

$$-6x - 30 = 6x - 30$$

$$-6x - 30 - 6x = 6x - 30 - 6x$$

$$-12x - 30 = -30$$

$$-12x - 30 + 30 = -30 + 30$$

$$-12x = 0$$

$$\frac{-12x}{-12} = \frac{0}{-12}$$

$$x = 0$$

◎ Pair/Share

How could you convince Michelle that there is a solution to this equation?

Solution: __No; There is one solution to this equation, $x = 0$.__

> How can you tell when a linear equation has no solution?

9 Draw lines to match each linear equation to its correct number of solutions.

Show your work.

$5(4 - x) = -5x + 20$ no solution

$-5(4 - x) = -5x + 20$ infinitely many solutions

$5(5 - x) = -5x + 20$ one solution

◎ Pair/Share

When the variable terms on both sides of an equation are the same, what does that tell you about the solution(s) to the equation?

10 Write a number in the box so that the equation will have the type of solution(s) shown.

no solution

$$\frac{1}{3}x + 5 = \frac{1}{3}x + \boxed{}$$

infinitely many solutions

$$\frac{1}{3}x + 5 = \frac{1}{3}x + \boxed{}$$

one solution

$$\frac{1}{3}x + 5 = \boxed{}x + 5$$

What is the difference between an equation with no solution and an equation with infinitely many solutions?

Pair/Share

What do you notice about the solution to equations that have the same variable term on each side of the equation?

11 What is the solution to the equation $3(x - 4) = 2(x - 6)$?

A $x = 0$

B $x = 1$

C There are infinitely many solutions.

D There is no solution.

Brian chose **D** as the correct answer. How did he get that answer?

_____

_____

_____

How can you simplify this equation to justify the correct answer?

Pair/Share

How could you explain the correct response to Brian?

Solve the problems.

1 How many solutions does the equation $2(2x - 10) - 8 = -2(14 - 3x)$ have?

A one solution

B two solutions

C no solution

D infinitely many solutions

2 How many solutions does the equation $10 - 3x + 10x - 7 = 5x - 5 + 2x + 8$ have?

A one solution

B two solutions

C no solution

D infinitely many solutions

3 For each linear equation in the table, shade in the appropriate box to indicate whether the equation has no solution, one solution, or infinitely many solutions.

Equation	No Solution	One Solution	Infinitely Many Solutions
$8x + 16 = 8x - 16$			
$-3x - 17 = -(17 + 3x)$			
$9x + 27 = 27$			
$2x - 6 = 6 + 2x$			

4 Which equation has an infinite number of solutions? Select all that apply.

A $3x - 2(x + 10) = x - 20$

B $5x + 2(x - 3) = 5x + 2(3 - x)$

C $\dfrac{x}{2} + 1 = \dfrac{3x}{10} + 3$

D $\dfrac{5}{2}x - 2 = \dfrac{9}{2}x - 2(x + 1)$

E $\dfrac{7}{2}x + x = x + \dfrac{7}{4}$

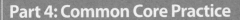

5 Consider the equation $2(5x - 4) = ax + b$.

Part A

Find a value for *a* and a value for *b* so that the equation has one solution. Explain your reasoning.

Show your work.

a = _____

b = _____

Part B

Find a value for *a* and a value for *b* so that the equation has no solution. Explain your reasoning.

Show your work.

a = _____

b = _____

Part C

Find a value for *a* and a value for *b* so that the equation has infinitely many solutions. Explain your reasoning.

Show your work.

a = _____

b = _____

✓ **Self Check** *Go back and see what you can check off on the Self Check on page 99.*

Lesson 15 Part 1: Introduction 👥

Understand Systems of Equations

> **How can graphs help you find the solution of two linear equations?**

In Lesson 14, you reviewed the structure of linear equations that have no solution, one solution, and infinitely many solutions. Now you will examine the graphs of pairs of linear equations to see if both equations have a common solution.

A **system of linear equations** is two or more related linear equations for which you are trying to find a common solution. The examples you will work within this lesson have two equations and two variables. To solve a system of equations, you need to find the ordered pair (or pairs) that solves both equations in the system. One way to find the solution is to graph the equations on the same coordinate plane.

🔍 **Think** Graphs of two linear equations might have no point of intersection.

Look at a graph of this system of equations.

$$y = 3x$$

$$y = 3x - 2$$

> **Circle the two variables that are used in this system of equations.**

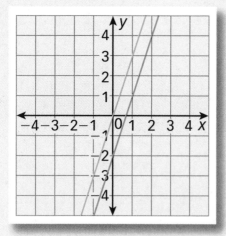

These lines don't intersect, so there is no ordered pair that will satisfy both equations. There is no point that lies on both lines. Like an equation that has no solution, this system has no solution.

Think Graphs of two linear equations might intersect in exactly one point.

Here is a graph of a system of equations with exactly one solution.

The point where the lines intersect, (0, 3), is a solution to both equations, so it solves the system. Like an equation that has exactly one solution, this system has exactly one solution. You can substitute (0, 3) into both equations to verify that it is a solution to both.

$y = -2x + 3$ $y = x + 3$

$3 = -2(0) + 3$ $3 = 0 + 3$

$3 = 3$ $3 = 3$

$y = -2x + 3$ and $y = x + 3$

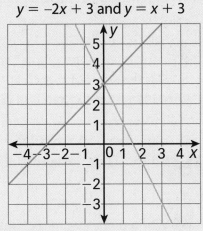

Think Graphs of two linear equations might intersect at all points.

Here is a graph of a system of equations with infinitely many solutions.

These two equations produce the same set of ordered pairs. When you substitute any value for x into each equation, you get the same y-values for each.

y + 2 = 2x				
x	−2	0	2	4
y	−6	−2	2	6

y = 2(x − 1)				
x	−2	0	2	4
y	−6	−2	4	6

$y + 2 = 2x$ and $y = 2(x - 1)$

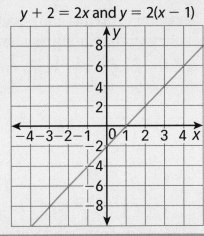

Reflect

1. Describe the number of solutions to a system of linear equations when the graph of the equations do not intersect, intersect in exactly one point, and intersect at all points.

_____

_____

_____

Explore It

Examining graphs and equations can help you determine if a system of linear equations has no solution.

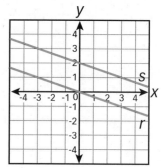

2 What are the slope and *y*-intercept of line *r* and line *s*?

_____

_____

3 Look back at the graph with no solution in the introduction. Are the slopes for each line the same or different? Are the *y*-intercepts the same or different?

_____

4 Why will these pairs of lines never intersect?

_____

5 When does a system of linear equations have no solution? Explain.

_____

_____

Examining graphs and equations can help you determine if a system of linear equations has infinitely many solutions.

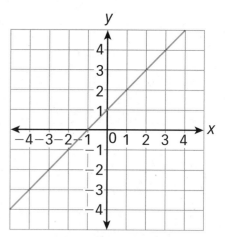

6 Substitute 4 and then −4 for *x* in the equations $y = x + 1$ and $2y - 2 = 2x$. Describe the results.

_____

_____

7 Divide each term in $2y - 2 = 2x$ by 2; then write it in slope-intercept form. _____

8 Now compare the equation you wrote in problem 7 with the first equation in problem 6.

_____

9 Find the system of equations in the introduction that has infinitely many solutions. Write each equation in slope-intercept form. Describe the results.

_____

_____

Talk About It

Solve the problems below as a group.

10 Look back at the system of equations in the introduction that has exactly one solution. Are the slopes of the two equations the same or different? Are the *y*-intercepts the same or different? _____

11 Compare the slopes and *y*-intercepts for the equations in this system of equations, and then graph the equations. How many solutions does this system of equations have?

$$y = x - 5$$

$$y = 2x - 5$$

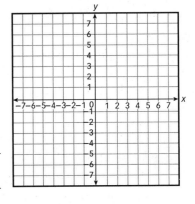

_____

_____

12 Each situation below describes a possible relationship between the equations in a system of equations. Write the number of solutions there are for each situation.

Equations with same slope and same *y*-intercept: _____

Equations with same slope and different *y*-intercepts: _____

Equations with different slopes and same *y*-intercept: _____

Equations with different slopes and different *y*-intercepts: _____

Try It Another Way

Examine each system of equations. Do both equations have the same slope or different slopes? The same *y*-intercept or different *y*-intercepts? Predict what kind of solution each one has. Justify your answers.

13 $y + 1 = \frac{1}{3}x$ _____

$y = \frac{1}{3}x$ _____

14 $y = 3x - 1$ _____

$y - 2 = \frac{1}{2}x$ _____

_____

Connect It

Talk through these problems as a class, then write your answers below.

15 **Analyze:** Look at the system of equations below. Without graphing, explain how you can tell what type of solution this system has.

$$y = \frac{1}{2}x + 3$$
$$y = 0.25(2x + 4)$$

_____

_____

_____

16 **Evaluate:** Look at the system of equations in the box at the right. Kevin stated that the equations in this system have the same slope, so there will be infinitely many solutions. Does Kevin's statement make sense? Explain.

System of Equations
$y = 1.5x + 4$
$y = 1.5x - 2$

_____

_____

_____

_____

17 **Create:** Study the graph at the right. Based on what you see, write an equation for each line. Substitute the coordinates of the point of intersection into both of your equations. Explain why this point is a solution of the system of equations.

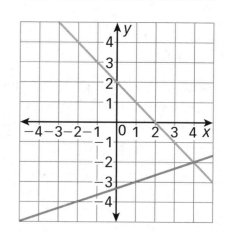

_____

_____

_____

_____

_____

Put It Together

18 Use what you have learned to complete this task.

Create a system of equations with the following number of solutions. Use the equation below as one of the equations in each system. Justify your answers.

$$y = \frac{1}{2}(6x - 8)$$

A exactly one solution

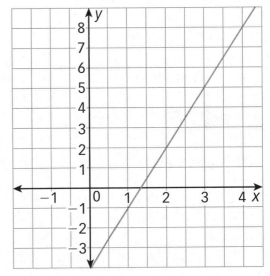

_____

_____

_____

_____

_____

_____

B infinitely many solutions

_____

_____

_____

C no solution

_____

_____

_____

_____

Lesson 16   Part 1: Introduction 👥

Solve Systems of Equations Algebraically

You know that solutions to systems of linear equations can be shown in graphs. Now you will learn about other ways to find the solutions. Take a look at this problem.

> Sienna wrote these equations to help solve a number riddle.
>
> $y = x - 20$
>
> $x + y = 84$
>
> What values for x and y solve both equations?

🔍 Explore It

Use math you already know to solve the problem.

- What does $y = x - 20$ tell you about the relationship between x and y?

  _____

- What does $x + y = 84$ tell you about the relationship between x and y?

  _____

- You can guess and check to solve the problem. Try 44 for x and 40 for y. Do these numbers solve both equations?

  _____

- Now try 50 for x. If $x = 50$, what is y when $y = x - 20$? Does that work with the other equation?

  _____

- Try $x = 52$. What do you find?

  _____

  _____

- Explain how you could find values for x and y that solve both equations.

  _____

🔍 Find Out More

In Lesson 15, you learned that without actually solving, you can tell if a system of equations will have exactly one solution, no solution, or infinitely many solutions. Here are some examples.

$x + y = 6$ $2x + 2y = 12$	The second equation is double the first one, so they are the same equation with the same graph and solution set. This system has infinitely many solutions.

$5x + y = 3$ $x = 4 - 5x$	If you write both equations in slope-intercept form, you find that $y = -5x + 4$ and $y = -5x + 3$. The lines have the same slope and different intercepts so they are parallel. This system has no solutions.

If a system of equations has exactly one solution, like the problem on the previous page, there are different ways you can find the solution.

You could guess and check, but that is usually not an efficient way to solve a system of equations. You could graph each equation, but sometimes you can't read an exact answer from the graph. Here is one way to solve the problem algebraically.

$y = x - 20$ $x + y = 84$	Substitute $x - 20$ for y in the second equation and solve for x. $x + (x - 20) = 84$ $2x - 20 = 84$ $2x = 104$ $x = 52$, so $y = 32$

You will learn more about algebraic methods later in the lesson.

✏️ Reflect

1 How does knowing $x = 52$ help you find the value of y?

_____

_____

_____

_____

Read the problem below. Then explore how to use substitution to solve systems of equations.

Solve this system of equations.

$y = x + 2$

$y + 1 = -4x$

Graph It

You can graph the equations and estimate the solution.

Find the point of intersection. It looks like

the solution is close to $\left(-\frac{1}{2}, 1\frac{1}{2}\right)$.

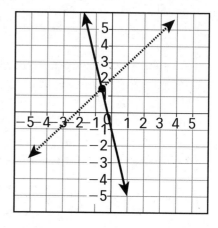

Model It

You can use substitution to solve for the first variable.

Notice that one of the equations tells you that $y = x + 2$. This allows you to use substitution to solve the system of equations.

Substitute $x + 2$ for y in the second equation.

$y = x + 2$

$y + 1 = -4x$

$(\boldsymbol{x + 2}) + 1 = -4x$

Now you can solve for x.

$x + 2 + 1 = -4x$

$x + 3 = -4x$

$3 = -5x$

$x = -\frac{3}{5}$

Connect It

Now you will solve for the second variable and analyze the solution.

2 What is the value of x? How can you find the value of y if you know the value of x?

_____

3 Substitute the value of x in the equation $y = x + 2$ to find the value of y.

_____

4 Now substitute the value of x in the equation $y = -4x - 1$ to find the value of y.

_____

5 What is the ordered pair that solves both equations? Where is this ordered pair located on the graph? _____

6 Look back at Model It. How does substituting $x + 2$ for y in the second equation give you an equation that you can solve? _____

_____

7 How does substitution help you to solve systems of equations? _____

_____

Try It

Use what you just learned to solve these systems of equations. Show your work on a separate sheet of paper.

8 $y - 3 = 2x$
$y = 4x - 2$

_____

9 $y = 1.4x + 2$
$y - 3.4x = -2$

_____

Read the problem below. Then explore how to solve systems of equations using elimination.

Solve this system of equations.

$-x - 2y = 4$

$3y = -0.5x + 2$

Model It

You can use elimination to solve for one variable.

First, write both equations so that like terms are in the same position. Then try to eliminate one of the variables, so you are left with one variable. To do this, look for a way to get opposite coefficients for one variable in the two equations.

$-2y = x + 4$

$3y = -0.5x + 2$

$2(3y = -0.5x + 2)$
$6y = \quad -x + 4$

- Multiply the second equation by 2. Now you have opposite terms: x in the first equation and $-x$ in the second equation.

$\begin{array}{r} -2y = \quad x + 4 \\ 6y = -x + 4 \\ \hline 4y = \qquad 8 \end{array}$

- Add the like terms in the two equations. The result is an equation in just one variable.

$y = 2$

- Divide each side by 4 to solve the equation for y.

$-2(2) = x + 4$
$-x - 4 = 4$
$\quad -x = 8$
$\quad\quad x = -8$

- Substitute the value of y into one of the original equations and solve for x.

Check:
$3(2) = -0.5(-8) + 2$
$\quad 6 = 4 + 2$

- Substitute your solution in the other original equation.

💡 Connect It

Now analyze the solution and compare methods for solving systems of equations.

10 What happens when you add opposites? Why do you want to get opposite coefficients for one of the variables? _____

_____

11 How did you get opposite coefficients for x in the solution on the previous page?

_____

12 Why does the equation stay balanced when you add the values on each side of the equal sign? _____

_____

_____

13 Which equation in the system was used to find the value of x? _____ Can you use the other equation? Explain. _____

_____

14 How is elimination like substitution? How is it different? _____

_____

_____

_____

15 How can you check your answer? _____

_____

✏️ Try It

Use what you just learned about elimination to solve this problem. Show your work on a separate sheet of paper.

16 $2x + y = 9$

$3x - y = 16$

Study the model below. Then solve problems 17–19.

The student divided each term in the equation $2y = 6x - 2$ by 2 to get an expression equal to y.

Student Model

Solve this system of equations.

$3y = x + 1$
$2y = 6x - 2$

Look at how you could use substitution to solve a system of equations.

$$\frac{2y = 6x - 2}{2}$$

$y = 3x - 1$

Since $y = 3x - 1$, I can substitute $3x - 1$ for y in the first equation.

$3(3x - 1) = x + 1$
$9x - 3 = x + 1$
$8x = 4$
$x = \frac{1}{2}$

$3y = \frac{1}{2} + 1; y = \frac{1}{2}$

Solution: $\left(\frac{1}{2}, \frac{1}{2}\right)$

Pair/Share

Solve the problem using elimination.

Can it help to write both equations in the same form?

17 What ordered pair is a solution to $y = x + 5$ and $x - 5y = -9$?

Show your work.

Pair/Share

Discuss your solution methods. Do you prefer using substitution or elimination?

Solution: _____

18 Graph the equations. What is your estimate of the solution of this system of equations?

$$y = 3x - 2$$
$$y = -2x$$

Show your work.

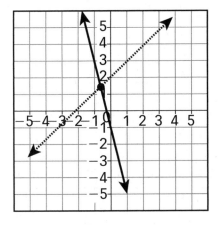

Solution: _____

Do the equations have the same or different slopes?

📎 Pair/Share

Solve the problem algebraically and compare the solution to your estimate.

19 Which of these systems of equations has no solution?

A $y = \frac{x}{4} + 2$

$y = 4x - 1$

B $y = \frac{2x}{3} - 3$

$y = 2x - 3$

C $y = 4x$

$y = 4x - 5$

D $x + y = 3$

$2y = -2x + 6$

Sheila chose **D** as the correct answer. How did she get that answer?

_____

_____

_____

What do you know about the lines in a system of equations with no solution?

📎 Pair/Share

Graph the solution to verify your answer.

Solve the problems.

1   Which statement about this system of equations is true?

$$y = \frac{1}{2}(8x + 4)$$

$$y - 4x = 2$$

A   It has no solution.

B   It has exactly one solution.

C   (0, 2) is the only solution.

D   It has infinitely many solutions.

2   For each pair of linear equations, shade in the box under the appropriate column to indicate whether the pair of equations has no solution, one solution, or infinitely many solutions.

Equations	No Solution	One Solution	Infinitely Many Solutions
$3x + 4y = 5$ $3x - 4y = 1$			
$y = 2x + 6$ $y = 2x - 9$			
$x - 3y = 7$ $2x - 6y = 14$			
$y = x$ $6x - y = 4$			

3   The graphs of lines *a* and *b* are shown on the coordinate plane. Match each line with its equation. Write the equation on the line provided for each line.

$y = 2x - 5$	$y = \frac{1}{3}x - 9$	$y = -\frac{1}{2}x + 5$
$y = 3x - 9$	$y = 2x + 5$	$y = -2x + 5$

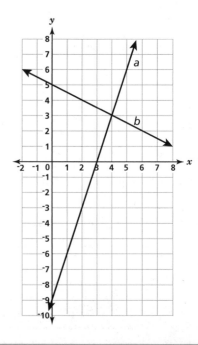

The equation of line *a* is _____ .

The equation of line *b* is _____ .

4 You know that the solution of a system of two linear equations is (−2, 1). Graph two lines that could be in this system of equations. Label the lines *a* and *b*. What has to be true about the graphs of both lines? What has to be different about the lines?

Show your work.

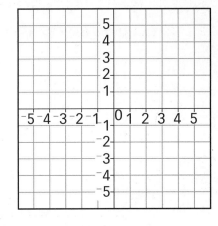

_____

_____

_____

_____

5 What is the equation of each line you drew in Problem 4? Explain how to check algebraically that your system of equations has a solution of (−2, 1).

Show your work.

_____

_____

_____

_____

 **Self Check** *Go back and see what you can check off on the Self Check on page 99.*

Lesson 17   Part 1: Introduction

Solve Problems Using Systems of Equations

You know how to solve systems of linear equations. Take a look at this problem.

> Mr. Torres spent $30.00 to buy $9\frac{1}{2}$ pounds of ground beef and chicken for a family cookout. If the price of ground beef was $3.50 per pound and chicken was $3.00 per pound, how many pounds of each did he buy?

🔍 Explore It

Use math you already know to solve the problem.

▨ Let b = pounds of ground beef and c = pounds of chicken.

▨ Write an equation that represents the weight of the ground beef and chicken together.

_____

▨ What other information is given in the problem?

_____

▨ How can you express the cost of the beef in terms of b and the cost of the chicken in terms of c?

_____

▨ Write a second equation to represent the total cost. _____

▨ Now write and solve a system of equations to solve the problem.

Find Out More

The key to solving real-world problems with systems of equations is to use the information given in the problem to write two related equations.

You know the total weight:

lb of beef + **lb of chicken** = total weight (9.5)

$$b + c = 9.5$$

You know the total cost:

cost of beef (3.5) · **lb of beef** + cost of chicken (3) · **lb of chicken** = total cost (30)

$$3.5b + 3c = 30$$

Both equations contain the same unknowns (b and c), and these unknowns must have the same value in each equation. That's why you can solve a system of equations to solve the problem.

Let's look at the ordered pair (5, 4.5), and verify that it solves both equations.

$b + c = 9.5$	$3.5b + 3c = 30$
$5 + 4.5 = 9.5$	$3.5(5) + 3(4.5) = 30$
	$17.50 + 13.50 = 30$

Reflect

1 Dan stocked up on batteries.

- He bought 14 packages of batteries for a total of 62 batteries.

- The AA batteries are sold in packages of 6, and the AAA batteries are sold in packages of 8.

Write a system of equations that can be solved to find how many packages of each type of battery Dan bought. Remember to define your variables.

_____

_____

_____

Read the problem below. Then explore different ways to solve a problem that can be represented by a system of equations.

> Bill and Brandon are downhill mountain-biking. Bill starts 500 feet ahead of Brandon and bikes at a rate of 42 feet per second. Brandon bikes at a rate of 50 feet per second. How long will it take Brandon to catch up to Bill?

Model It

You can write a system of equations to model the problem.

Bill and Brandon are biking at different rates. They started at the same time but at different locations. You need to find the point where they meet.

You can think of this as traveling equal distances, but you need to account for the fact that one biker started a certain distance ahead of the other.

Use this formula: rate • time = distance

Brandon: $50 \cdot t = d$

Bill: $42 \cdot t = d - 500$

Graph It

You can graph the equations to estimate the solution.

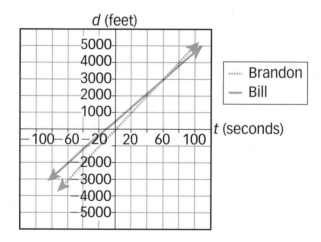

Connect It

Now you solve a system of equations to solve the problem.

2 Use the graph to estimate the point where Bill and Brandon meet. Will their times be the same at the meeting point? Will the distances they travelled be the same? Explain.

_____

_____

_____

_____

3 Fill in the blanks to explain what the two equations represent.

Brandon bikes at _____ feet per second for a certain amount of _____ and travels a certain _____.

Bill bikes at _____ feet per second for the same amount of _____ and travels _____ feet _____ than Brandon does.

4 Describe how the graph represents the problem situation.

_____

_____

5 Solve the system of equations algebraically. Then, describe what the solution means in the context of the problem.

_____

_____

Try It

Use what you just learned to solve this problem. Show your work on a separate sheet of paper.

6 Membership at Ace Gym is $30 per month plus a one-time registration fee of $100. Membership at Bold's Gym is $50 per month, and there is no registration fee. After how many months will the membership costs be the same at both gyms?

_____

_____

Study the model below. Then solve problems 7–9.

The student uses the slope formula to find the slope of each line.

Student Model

Line *a* passes through the points (2, 1) and (1, −1). Line *b* passes through the points (−3, −2) and (−1, 0). Do lines *a* and *b* intersect? Justify your answer.

Look at how you could show your work.

Find the slope of each line.

Line *a*: $\dfrac{-1-1}{1-2} = \dfrac{-2}{-1}$ or 2

Line *b*: $\dfrac{0-(-2)}{-1-(-3)} = \dfrac{2}{2}$ or 1

The lines have different slopes, so they will intersect at exactly one point.

Solution: ___Lines *a* and *b* intersect.___

Pair/Share

What would the student have needed to do if the slopes were equal? Why?

Writing equations for the plans might help you compare them.

7 Nicky is considering two different companies for textbook rentals. For what number of months will Company B cost less?

• Company A charges a one-time account fee of $20 and a rental fee of $15 per month.

• Company B charges $20 per month with no other fees.

Show your work.

Pair/Share

Describe the situation in which Company A would be a better deal.

Solution: _____

8 Gina visited the aquarium with some of her cousins, aunts, and uncles. The group bought 20 admission tickets for $340. Adult tickets cost $20, and children's tickets cost $15. How many adult and children's tickets did the group buy?

Show your work.

What do the two given totals represents?

Pair/Share

How can you check that your answer is correct? Check your partner's answer.

Solution: _____

9 A telephone plan costs $42 per month plus $0.08 per minute of calls made. Another plan costs $50 per month plus $0.05 per minute of calls made. Which system of equations could you use to compare the monthly cost of the plans?

A $c = 42 - 0.08m$

$c = 50 - 0.05m$

B $c = 42m + 0.08$

$c = 50m + 0.05$

C $c = 42 + 0.05m$

$c = 50 + 0.08m$

D $c = 42 + 0.08m$

$c = 50 + 0.05m$

Casey chose **B** as the correct answer. How did he get that answer?

_____

_____

What part of the monthly bill changes? What part stays the same?

Pair/Share

How would you explain to Casey why his answer is incorrect?

Solve the problems.

1 One number is 16 more than another number. The two numbers have a sum of 120. Which system of equations could you use to find the two numbers?

A $y = x - 16$
$y = x + 120$

B $y = x + 16$
$y = x + 120$

C $y = x - 16$
$y = x - 120$

D $y = x - 16$
$y = -x + 120$

2 Which point lies on the line $2y - 3x = 4$? Select Yes or No for each point.

A (4, 8) ☐ Yes ☐ No

B (12, 24) ☐ Yes ☐ No

C (6, 11) ☐ Yes ☐ No

D (−2, −1) ☐ Yes ☐ No

E (−4, −2) ☐ Yes ☐ No

3 Line *a* passes through (2, 3) and (6, 5) on a coordinate plane. Lines *b*, *c*, and *d* are defined by the ordered pairs below.

• Line *b* passes through (−2, 1) and (4, 4).

• Line *c* passes through (8, 6) and (−1, −3).

• Line *d* passes through (−4, 2) and (2, 5).

Determine whether lines *b*, *c*, and *d* form lines that intersect line *a* at no points, one point, or an infinite number of points. Write the name of the line in the appropriate box.

No points of intersection with line *a*.	One point of intersection with line *a*.	Infinite points of intersection with line *a*.

4 Two taxi companies charge different rates.

   Metro Taxi: $3.00 for the first mile and $2.50 for each additional mile

   City Taxi: $5.00 for the first mile and $2.25 for each additional mile

Part A

For how many additional miles and how many total miles would the charge be the same at each company?

Show your work.

Answer _____

Part B

Use the table below to describe a situation in which it would make more sense to use Metro Taxi. Then, describe a different situation in which it would make more sense to use City Taxi. Explain your answer.

Show your work.

Miles	1	2	3	4	5	6	7	8	9	10
Metro Taxi	3	5.5	8	10.5	13	15.5	18	20.5	23	25.5
City Taxi	5	7.25	9.5	11.75	14	16.25	18.5	20.75	23	25.25

_____

_____

 **Self Check**   *Go back and see what you can check off on the Self Check on page 99.*

Solve the problems.

1 Chad's pay rate for babysitting is $y = 9x$, where x is the number of hours he babysits, and y is the number of dollars he earns. Horatio's pay rate is shown in the graph below.

Horatio's Babysitting Pay Rate

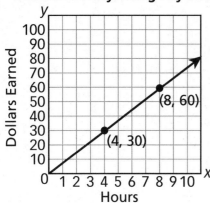

Which of the following statements is true?

A Chad makes $1.00 more per hour than Horatio.

B Chad makes $1.50 more per hour than Horatio.

C Chad makes $1.00 less per hour than Horatio.

D Chad makes $1.50 less per hour than Horatio.

2 Which equation forms a pair of linear equations with $9x + 12y = 48$ such that the system has no solution?

A $16x - 12y = -48$

B $6x + 12y = -48$

C $3x + 4y = 12$

D $6x + 8y = 32$

3 In the graph below, the slopes of $\overline{AC}$ and $\overline{CE}$ are the same.

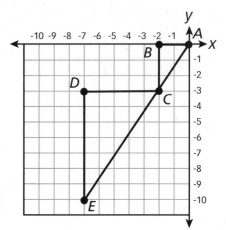

What conclusion can be made about triangle *ABC* and triangle *CDE*?

A They are congruent.

B They are equilateral.

C They are similar.

D They are collinear.

4 Lynn solved a system of linear equations and got $8 = 8$. Which statement about this system is true? Select all that apply.

A x must equal 8.

B y must equal 8.

C The graphs of the two equations coincide.

D There is no solution to the system.

E There are infinitely many solutions to the system.

F The point (8, 8) is the solution to the system.

5 What is the solution to $\frac{3}{5}(4x - 5) + 4\frac{1}{2} = \frac{1}{4}x - 9\frac{1}{4}$?

Show your work.

Answer _____

6 Graph the system of linear equations on a coordinate plane.

$$2x - 3y = -9$$
$$3x + y = -8$$

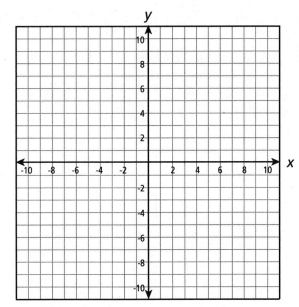

What is the solution to the system of linear equations?

Answer _____

Performance Task

Answer the questions and show all your work on separate paper.

Your friend Sharleen is thinking about joining an online gaming club. She's trying to decide between *Multiplayer Madness* and *Games Galore*. Her brother insists that *Multiplayer Madness* is a better deal.

Multiplayer Madness charges a joining fee of $50. It's a bit more expensive than *Games Galore*, a club that charges a $10 joining fee. But, *Multiplayer Madness* only charges a fee of $15 a month. That's $5 less each month than the fee charged at *Games Galore*!

Sharleen got out her calculator and found that 3 months would cost $70 at *Multiplayer Madness*, but would cost $95 at *Games Galore*. Maybe her brother is right for a change.

Sharleen is considering joining for either 3 months, 8 months, or 12 months. Will the costs for the two clubs ever be the same? Is one a better deal? Write a summary of the costs for each club and give Sharleen advice on which one she should choose. Include a graph with your explanation.

> ☑ **CHECKLIST**
>
> Did you . . .
>
> ☐ Write expressions to represent the costs of each club?
>
> ☐ Draw a graph?
>
> ☐ Justify your advice to Sharleen?

Reflect on Mathematical Practices

After you complete the task, choose one of the following questions to answer.

1. **Persevere** Have you solved a problem like this before? How did that help you decide on a plan?

2. **Model** How did drawing a graph help you advise Sharleen on which gaming plan she should buy?

Derek projected a picture he drew of Martin Luther King, Jr. onto the school cafeteria wall. Is this projection an exact copy of Derek's original picture? He used the same picture and projected a second copy next to the first. Are these two pictures the same? Derek then flipped the picture upside down and projected it on the opposite wall. Are the three projected pictures exact copies of each other?

In this unit, you will examine angles and side lengths of two-dimensional figures and decide whether or not they are exact copies or are similar to one another. You will also use the Pythagorean Theorem to find side lengths of right triangles and use formulas to find the volume of three-dimensional figures.

✓ Self Check

Before starting this unit, check off the skills you know below. As you complete each lesson, see how many more you can check off!

I can:	Before this unit	After this unit
demonstrate the properties of translations, rotations, and reflections	☐	☐
give the new coordinates of a figure in the coordinate plane after a translation, rotation, or reflection	☐	☐
identify pairs of congruent angles when a transversal intersects parallel lines	☐	☐
identify similar triangles based on angle measurements	☐	☐
demonstrate why the sum of the angle measures in any triangle is 180°	☐	☐
explain a proof of the Pythagorean Theorem	☐	☐
apply the Pythagorean Theorem to solve problems	☐	☐

Lesson 18 Part 1: Introduction 👥

Understand Properties of Transformations

CCSS
8.G.A.1a
8.G.A.1b
8.G.A.1c

What are different ways a figure can be moved?

There are three ways to move a figure from one place to another. These movements are called **transformations**.

1. You can slide the figure.

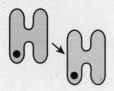

2. You can reflect the figure.

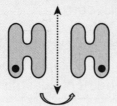

3. You can rotate the figure.

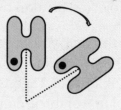

🔍 Think   What is a translation?

A **translation**, or slide, moves every point of a figure the same distance and in the same direction. The figure moves left, right, up, or down. Here are some examples of translations.

Circle the words that describe how a figure moves in a translation.

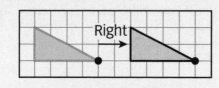

Right

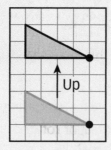

Up

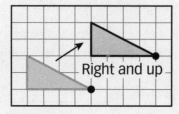

Right and up

🔍 **Think**   What is a reflection?

A **reflection**, or flip, flips a figure over an imaginary line that can be horizontal, vertical, or slanted. The line is called a **line of reflection**. Imagine folding on the line of reflection. The original figure and its image would match exactly. Corresponding points on the original figure and its image are the same distance from the line of reflection. Here are some examples of reflections.

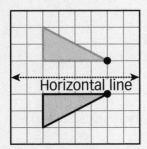
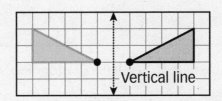
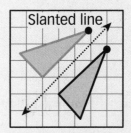

🔍 **Think**   What is a rotation?

A **rotation**, or turn, moves a figure around a fixed point. The fixed point is called the **center of rotation**. The figure turns in either a clockwise or counterclockwise direction. Here are some examples of rotations.

A 360° rotation turns a full circle.

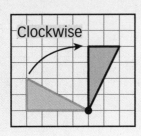
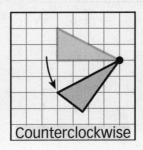

✏️ **Reflect**

1   When a figure is translated, reflected, or rotated, what's the same about the original figure and its image? What's different?

_____

_____

_____

Explore It

Analyzing a figure and its image can help you understand the properties of transformations.

The figure on the right is a transformation of the figure on the left. Each square represents 1 unit.

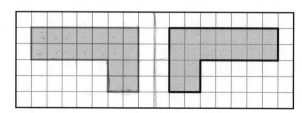

2 Is the transformation a translation, reflection, or rotation? Explain your reasoning.

The transformation is a reflection because the figure on the right is a mirror reflection of the figure on the left.

3 How do the lengths of the sides in the original figure compare to the lengths of the sides in its image? How do you know?

The lengths of the sides in the original Figure compare to the lengths of the sides because they have seven units length top and they have the same distance from the y axis.

4 Describe the angles in the original figure. _The angles in the original are 90 degrees angle_

Describe the angles in the image. _The angles are 90 degrees angles too_

5 Are any of the sides of the original figure parallel? _Yes_

Are any of the sides parallel in the image? _Yes_

Now try this problem.

6 Use a separate sheet of paper to trace the green figure shown. Cut out the figure. Use your cutout to decide how you could move the green figure to get each gray figure. Write the letter of the figure that matches the transformation and then complete the problem.

Translation _C_ Describe the move. _The green figure_
move down but it didn't change direction

Reflection _A_ Draw the line of reflection.

Rotation _B_ Draw the point that is the center of rotation.

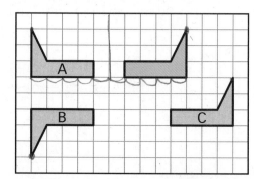

💬 Talk About It

Solve the problems below as a group.

7 Look at your answers to problems 3–5 on the previous page. What properties of a figure's lines and angles remain the same when you reflect the figure?

_____

_____

8 Trace the green hexagon at the top of the previous page. Cut out the figure. Use the cutout and a separate sheet of paper to create translations and rotations of the figure. What properties of a figure's lines and angles remain the same when you translate or rotate the figure?

_____

_____

✏️ Try It Another Way

Work with your group to explore properties of a rotation using rulers and protractors.

The gray triangle is a rotation of the green triangle.

9 Measure the lengths of the sides of △ABC to the nearest cm and measure the angles to the nearest degree.

$AB =$ _5 cm_ $BC =$ _4 cm_ $AC =$ _3 cm_

$\angle A =$ _53°_ $\angle ABC =$ _38°_ $\angle C =$ _96°_

10 Measure the lengths of the sides of △XBY to the nearest cm and measure the angles to the nearest degree.

$XB =$ _5_ $BY =$ _4_ $YX =$ _3_

$\angle X =$ _53°_ $\angle XBY =$ _____ $\angle Y =$ _____

11 Compare the triangles. What can you say about the lengths of the sides and the measures of the angles of the two triangles?

The lengths of the sides are the same because they are the same measurements

because they are the same shape

Connect It

Talk through these problems as a class, then write your answers below.

12 Explain: Tell whether the gray figure appears to be a reflection of the green figure. Explain why or why not.

a.

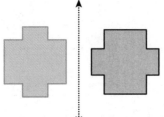

b.

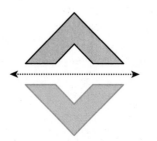

c.

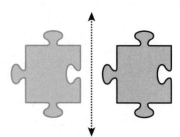

No the gray figure is not a reflection of the green figure its rotation because the figure turned in a different direction

Yes the green figure is reflection because everything stays the same its just the green figure flips the oppsite way of the original figure.

No the gray figure is not a reflection its translation because it just changes position not give it

13 Draw: Imagine spinning this flag clockwise around in a circle about point *O*. Draw a 90° rotation, a 180° rotation, and a 270° rotation. Use a different color for each rotation.

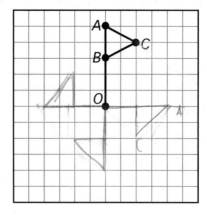

14 Analyze: Refer back to the rotated flag in Problem 13. What is always true about $\overline{OA}$ and $\overline{OB}$ in each of the images of rotation?

They are the same length and size

💡 Put It Together

15 Use what you have learned to complete this task.

Alan created each design by moving the same triangle in different ways and tracing it after each move.

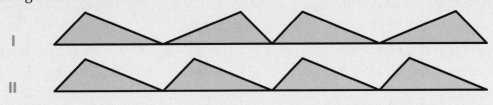

A Identify the type of transformation that created the designs shown above.

I _____   II _____

B Choose a different figure and make your own design on the grid below using one type of transformation. Describe how you moved the figure to make your design.

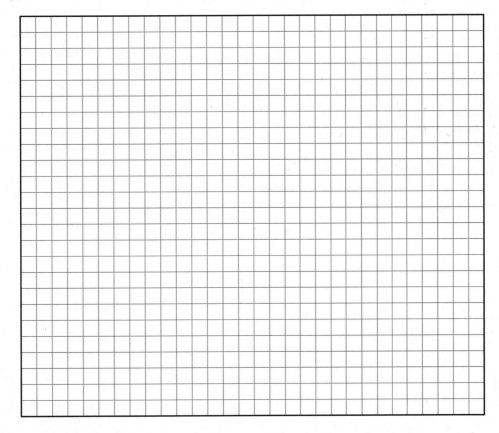

_____

_____

Lesson 19   Part 1: Introduction 👥

Transformations and Congruence

You learned about different types of transformations. In this lesson you will learn about the relationship between the image and the pre-image of a transformation. Take a look at this problem.

Alexia is making right triangles to decorate the border of a poster. She traced around a triangle template on graph paper. Then she translated the template 5 units to the right and 1 unit up, and traced it again. She labeled the original figure, or pre-image $\triangle ABC$ and the image $\triangle PQR$.

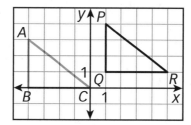

What is the relationship between $\triangle ABC$ and $\triangle PQR$?

🔍 Explore It

Use the math you already know to solve this problem.

⬤ Remember that when a segment is reflected, translated, or rotated, its length stays the same. Find the lengths of $\overline{AB}$, $\overline{BC}$, $\overline{PQ}$, and $\overline{QR}$. Which segments have equal lengths?

_____

⬤ Which segment in $\triangle PQR$ do you think is the same length as AC? _____

⬤ When an angle is reflected, translated, or rotated, its measure stays the same. Which angle in $\triangle PQR$ has the same measure as $\angle B$? _____

⬤ Which other angles in the triangles do you think have the same measure? Why?

_____

_____

_____

Find Out More

The triangles in the diagram on the previous page, △ABC and △PQR, are *congruent*. This is written △ABC ≅ △PQR. The symbol ≅ is read "is congruent to."

Two segments are **congruent** if they are the same length. In this diagram, $\overline{HK} \cong \overline{YZ}$.

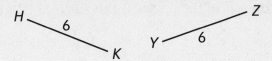

Two angles are **congruent** if they are the same measure. In this diagram, ∠P ≅ ∠C.

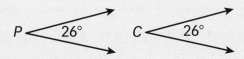

Two polygons are **congruent** if all of their corresponding sides are congruent and all of their corresponding angles are congruent.

These two triangles are not congruent because they appear to have congruent angles, but do not have congruent sides.	These two triangles are congruent because their corresponding sides are congruent and their corresponding angles are congruent.

Reflect

1 Use what you know about properties of transformations to explain why △LMO is congruent to △NMO.

_____

_____

_____

_____

_____

_____

Read the problem below. Then use what you know about rotations to explore congruent polygons.

The coordinates of the vertices of $\triangle ABC$ are $A(2, 1)$, $B(2, 5)$, and $C(4, 5)$. $\triangle ABC$ is rotated 180° counterclockwise about the origin.

What are the coordinates of the vertices of the image of $\triangle ABC$?

Are $\triangle ABC$ and its image congruent? Explain how you know.

Graph It

You can graph the triangle and its image to help solve the problem.

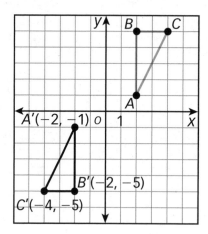

Model It

You can use what you know about transformations to describe the relationship between the two triangles.

$\overline{AB} \cong \overline{A'B'}$ $\overline{AC} \cong \overline{A'C'}$ $\overline{BC} \cong \overline{B'C'}$

Each side of the triangle is congruent to a side of its image.

$\angle A \cong \angle A'$ $\angle B \cong \angle B'$ $\angle C \cong \angle C'$

Each angle of the triangle is congruent to an angle of its image.

All of the sides and angles of $\triangle ABC$ are congruent to the corresponding parts of $\triangle A'B'C'$.

Connect It

Now you will find out if a polygon is congruent to its image using different transformations.

2 Explain why $\triangle ABC \cong \triangle A'B'C'$.

_____

_____

3 Sketch $\triangle ABC$ from the previous page and reflect it in the *x*-axis. Is the image of $\triangle ABC$ congruent to the original figure? Explain why or why not.

_____

4 Sketch $\triangle ABC$ from the previous page. Sketch the image of the triangle after a translation 3 units up and 4 units to the left. Is the image of $\triangle ABC$ congruent to its pre-image? Explain why or why not.

_____

5 Janice says that translations, rotations, and reflections may move a polygon around, but don't change its shape or size. Do you agree with her? Explain why or why not.

_____

_____

Try It

Use what you just learned about transformations and congruence to solve this problem. Show your work on a separate sheet of paper.

6 Polygon *A* is the result of reflecting Polygon *B* in the line $y = 2$. Explain how you know that the two polygons are congruent.

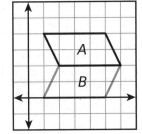

_____

_____

_____

Read the problem below. Then explore how to describe a transformation that maps a polygon to a congruent polygon.

In the diagram below, $\triangle ZWO \cong \triangle YXO$. Describe the transformation that transforms $\triangle ZWO$ to $\triangle YXO$.

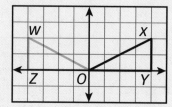

Model It

You can describe with words how the coordinates of each vertex change.

$(-4, 0)$ is transformed to $(4, 0)$.

$(-4, 2)$ is transformed to $(4, 2)$.

$(0, 0)$ is transformed to $(0, 0)$.

Picture It

You can make a diagram that shows how the vertices of the triangles correspond to help you solve the problem.

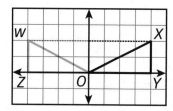

Z is transformed to Y.

W is transformed to X.

O is transformed to *itself*.

Connect It

7 What kind of transformation is used to transform △ZWO to △YXO? Explain.

_____

_____

8 Write and then compare the coordinate pairs for corresponding vertices.
What do you notice?

Z (_____)   Y (_____)   W (_____)   X (_____)

_____

9 How does your answer to problem 8 fit with the locations of vertices of the original
figure and its reflection image?

_____

_____

10 How does a reflection of an image over the *y*-axis change the coordinates of the vertices?

_____

_____

Try It

**Use what you just learned about coordinates of transformations to
solve these problems.**

11 Sketch a translation of △ZWO from the previous page by moving it
2 units right and 1 unit up. Label the translation image △Z′W′O′.
Write the coordinates below.

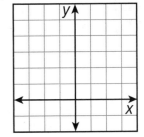

Z (_____)   Z′ (_____)

W (_____)   W′ (_____)

O (_____)   O′ (_____)

12 Compare the corresponding vertices. What do you notice about the difference in
x-values? in *y*-values?

_____

_____

Study the student model below. Then solve problems 13–15.

The student sees that △JHK looks like a reflection of △ZWO, but it needs to be transformed again.

There is no single transformation that transforms △ZWO to △JHK. Describe two different transformations that can be used in a sequence to transform △ZWO to △JHK.

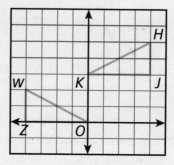

Reflect △ZWO over the *y*-axis. Then move it up 3 units. It will be

at the exact location of △JHK.

💬**Pair/Share**

Does it work to reverse the order of the two transformations? Do you think this will always be true?

What type of transformation moves a polygon but keeps its orientation the same?

13 Describe a transformation or a series of transformations that transforms *PQRS* to *JKLM*.

Show your work.

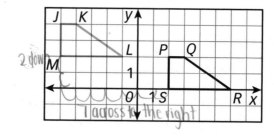

💬**Pair/Share**

If the original figure is *JKLM* and the image is *PQRS*, how would your answer be different?

Solution: Translation; we moved 2 down and 7 units to the right

14 Transform ΔDEF by reflecting it in the *y*-axis, and label the image ΔPQR. Transform ΔPQR by reflecting it in the *x*-axis, and label the new image ΔUVW. What is a single transformation that transforms ΔDEF to ΔUVW?

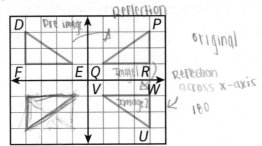

The image from the first transformation is the original figure of the second transformation.

Solution: ___rotation of 180°___

Pair/Share
Can you think of more than one single transformation that will transform ΔDEF to ΔPQR?

15 Which transformation transforms ΔLMO to ΔNPO?

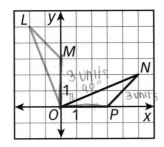

Does ΔLMO appear to have been rotated, reflected, or translated?

A Translation three units right

B 180° rotation counterclockwise

C 90° rotation clockwise

D Reflection in the *y*-axis

Aliya chose **A** as her answer. How did she get that answer?

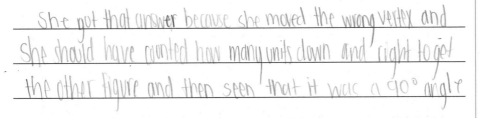

___She got that answer because she moved the wrong vertex and she should have counted how many units down and right to get the other figure and then seen that it was a 90° angle___

Pair/Share
Explain what the correct answer should be.

Solve the problems.

1 To show that *A* and *B* are congruent rectangles, which transformation or series of transformations could you use?

A   Rotation of 180° about the origin

B   Translation 4 units right and 1 unit up

C   Reflection in the *x*-axis, followed by a reflection in the *y*-axis

D   All of the above

2 Tricia plotted the point (4, 2) on a coordinate plane. She then performed a series of transformations on the point so that the point mapped onto its original location of (4, 2). Sort the transformations below so that (4, 2) maps onto itself by the end of the last transformation. Write the correct transformation for each step.

| Dilation of $\frac{1}{2}$ with the center of dilation at the origin |

| Translation 2 units right and 3 units up |

| Reflection over the *y*-axis |

| Rotation 180° |

Step 1	
Step 2	
Step 3	
Step 4	

3 During math class, Thomas draws a triangle on a coordinate plane. He is going to draw four transformations of the triangle. For each transformation listed below, decide whether a new image is always, sometimes, or never congruent to the original image. Write the name of the transformation in the correct column.

Transformation	Always congruent to the original image	Sometimes congruent to the original image	Never congruent to the original image
Translation Reflection Rotation Dilation	Translation Reflection Rotation	Dilation	

4 Describe at least two different ways to transform A to B.

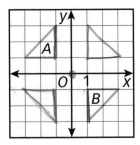

· Rotated 180° and reflection across the x-axis and the y-axis.

5 Jeremy says that if you translate, rotate, or reflect a polygon, the area of the image is the same as the area of the original figure. Do you agree or disagree? Explain your choice.

I agree because even if you rotate, translate, or reflect a polygon the area of the image is the same as the area of the orignal figure because the size and shape doesn't change it stays the same.

✓ **Self Check** *Go back and see what you can check off on the Self Check on page 159.*

Lesson 20 Part 1: Introduction 👥

Transformations and Similarity

You learned that if you reflect, translate, or rotate a shape, the figure and its image are congruent. In this lesson you will learn about a transformation that changes the size of a polygon.

Michael is using a photo editing program to adjust the size of photos for a yearbook. To avoid distorting the image, he pulls a corner of the photo along a line, as shown by the dotted line.

What type of transformation transforms △*OAB* to △*OCD*?

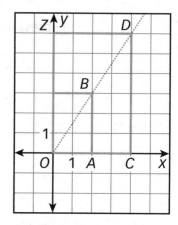

🔍 Explore It

Use the math you already know to solve this problem.

■ Find the lengths of segments *OA*, *AB*, *OC*, and *CD*. What do you notice about the lengths of corresponding sides?

OA=2 AB=3 OC=4 CD=6

■ Compare the coordinates of the vertices of △*OAB* and △*OCD*. What do you notice about the coordinates? _____

_____

_____

■ Remember that the lengths of corresponding sides of similar triangles are in proportion. Are △*OAB* and △*OCD* similar triangles? Explain why or why not.

_____

_____

🔍 Find Out More

The transformation that transforms △OAB to △OCD is called a *dilation*. A **dilation** is a transformation in which the original figure and the image are similar. — Same: but not exactly the same size

In a dilation, the ratio of the length of a side of the original figure to the length of the corresponding side of the image is called the **scale factor**. The **center** of a dilation is the point that is transformed to itself by the dilation.

In the dilation on the previous page, the ratio $\frac{OC}{OA}$ is $\frac{4}{2}$ and the ratio $\frac{DC}{BA}$ is $\frac{6}{3}$. So the scale factor is 2. The center of dilation is the origin, or point O.

In this lesson, you will work with scale factors greater than 0. If the scale factor of the dilation is greater than 1, the image is larger in size than the original figure. If the scale factor is between 0 and 1, the image is smaller in size than the original figure.

✏️ Reflect

1   Write the coordinates of the image of the parallelogram below after a dilation with scale factor 3 and center O. _____

_____

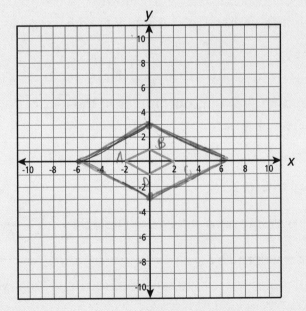

A(−2,0)   A'(−2·3, 0·3)
B(0,1)   A'(−6,0)
C(2,0)   B'(0·3, 1·3)
D(0,−1)   B'(0,3)
          C'(2·3, 0·3)
          C'(6, 0)
          D'(0·3, −1·3)
          D'(0, −3)

Read the problem below. Then learn about combining a dilation with another transformation.

In the diagram below, △PQR is similar to △LMN. Describe the sequence of transformations that transform △PQR to △LMN.

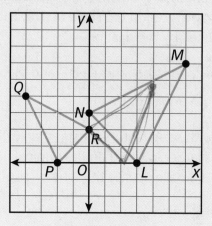

Model It

You can describe the transformation with words.

△PQR was flipped, or reflected, over the y-axis.

△PQR was increased in size, or dilated about center O, with a scale factor of $\frac{3}{2}$.

Model It

You can describe the change in the coordinates of the vertices of the triangle.

P(−2, 0) was transformed to L (3, 0).

Q(−4, 4) was transformed to M (6, 6).

R(0, 2) was transformed to N (0, 3).

Each x-coordinate has opposite signs and was multiplied by $\frac{3}{2}$.

Each y-coordinate was multiplied by $\frac{3}{2}$.

💡 Connect It

Now you will explore how to combine a dilation with another transformation.

2 What line of reflection is used to transform △PQR to △LMN? Explain.

The line of reflection that is used to transform △PQR to △LMN is the
y-axis because if it were the x-axis

3 What scale factor and center is used to transform △PQR to △LMN? Explain.

The scale factor is 3 and the center that is used is 0 because it never changes.

4 Does it matter if △PQR is first dilated, then reflected, or if it is first reflected, then dilated? Explain why or why not.

It does matter because we would get different coordinates if
we would have first dilated and then reflected.

5 Suppose △LMN is the original figure and △PQR is the image of the sequence of transformations. Would this change the description of the transformations?

The description of the transformations would not change

6 Problem 5 shows that a dilation with a scale factor between 0 and 1 shrinks the polygon. What do you think is the effect of a dilation with a scale factor of 1?

If the dilation is equal to one, then there is no change in size because 1 is
it is equal.

Y
P(-2,0) Q(-4,4) R(0,2)

ransformation or sequence of transformations

axis and dilated by

We used
the scale
factor 3/2
& multiplied (6,3) V'(2,2) U(-6,0)
our points
from △ U'(0,2)
PQR in
quadrant 2 3·1 1
_6 2 2_

Rotate across y-axis 90°
dilated

L(-3,0) M(-6,6) N(0,3)

179

Study the student model below. Then solve problems 8–10.

The student reflected the triangle across the x-axis, then multiplied each of the coordinates by $\frac{1}{2}$.

$\triangle ABC$ is reflected across the *x*-axis and dilated with scale factor $\frac{1}{2}$ and center *O*. What are the coordinates of the vertices of the image of $\triangle ABC$?

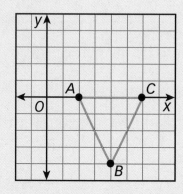

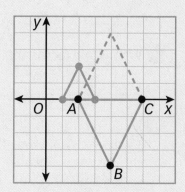

Solution: The coordinates of the vertices of the final image are

(1, 0); (3, 0); and (2, 2).

🗨 **Pair/Share**

How else could you make these transformations?

---

8 The coordinates of the vertices of $\triangle OPQ$ are *O*(0, 0); *P*(4, 0); and *Q*(2, −4). $\triangle OPQ$ is dilated with center *O* and scale factor $\frac{3}{2}$. Sketch the dilation. What quadrant or quadrants contains the image of $\triangle OPQ$?

Show your work.

Start by graphing $\triangle OPQ$.

O (0,0)
Q (2,-4)
R (4,0)

Dilation $\frac{3}{2} = 1\frac{1}{2}$

$\rightarrow (0 \cdot \frac{3}{2}, 0 \cdot \frac{3}{2})$ O'(0,0)
$\rightarrow (+2 \cdot \frac{3}{2}, -4 \cdot \frac{3}{2})$ Q'(-3,-6)
$\rightarrow (+4 \cdot \frac{3}{2}, 0 \cdot \frac{3}{2})$ P'(6,0)

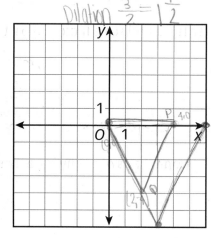

🗨 **Pair/Share**

Do you think a dilation with center (0, 0) moves a polygon from one quadrant to another quadrant?

Solution: Both images are on the same quadrant, 4.

---

9 The coordinates of the vertices of a trapezoid are (0, 0), (2, 4), (5, 4), and (7, 0). The trapezoid is dilated with scale factor 2 and center (0, 0). What are the coordinates of the vertices of the image of the trapezoid?

$(0,0) = (0,0) =$
$(2,4) = (4,8)$
$(5,4) \quad (10,8)$
$(7,0) \quad (14,0)$

When the center of dilation is at the origin, what effect does the scale factor have on the coordinates?

Solution: $(0,0), (4,8), (10,8), (14,0)$

Pair/Share

Did you need to make a sketch for this problem?

10 What two transformations could transform the smaller square to the larger square?

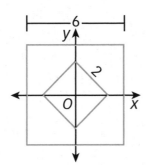

Make sure you consider both the scale factor and degree of rotation as you look for the correct answer.

A Dilation with center *O* and scale factor 3; rotation 45° about *O*

B Dilation with center *O* and scale factor 3; rotation 90° about *O*

C Dilation with center *O* and scale factor $\frac{1}{3}$; rotation 45° about *O*

D Dilation with center *O* and scale factor $\frac{1}{3}$; rotation 180° about *O*

Hattie chose **C** as the correct answer. Why is her answer incorrect?

_____

_____

_____

_____

Pair/Share

Why is the order in the description of a dilation important?

Solve the problems.

1 An equilateral triangle with side length 1.5 is dilated with a scale factor of 4. What is the length of one side of the image of the triangle?

A   0.375

B   3

C   1.5

D   6

2 Triangle *ABC* is shown on the coordinate plane. Shade in the points that represent the vertices of triangle *A'B'C'* after a dilation using a scale factor of 2 with the center of dilation at the origin. Then, connect the vertices *A'*, *B'*, *C'* to form the new triangle.

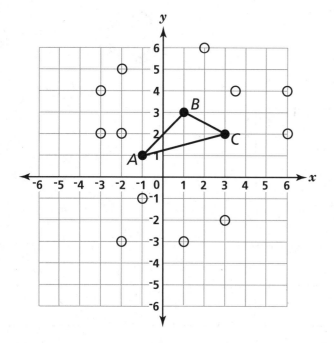

3 On the coordinate plane below, triangle *ABC* was rotated 180 degrees around the origin and then dilated by a factor of 2 with the center of dilation at the origin to form the green triangle, where *x*, *y*, and *z* represent the side lengths of the green triangle.

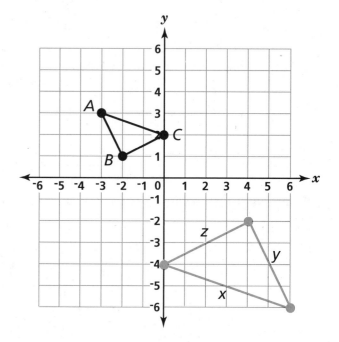

Complete the equality below by entering *x*, *y*, or *z* in the appropriate denominator.

$$\frac{AB}{\Box} = \frac{BC}{\Box} = \frac{AC}{\Box}$$

4 Describe at least two different transformations or sequences of transformations that transform square *A* to square *B*.

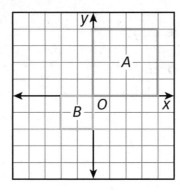

_____

_____

5 Sketch a trapezoid on a coordinate plane, then choose two dilations with different scale factors. Draw the image of the trapezoid after each dilation. Are the sides of the trapezoid that are parallel in the original figure parallel in the image? Do you think that your result will be true for any dilation? Explain why or why not.

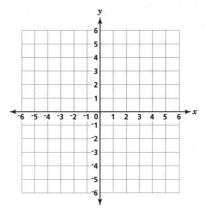

_____

_____

_____

_____

✓ **Self Check** *Go back and see what you can check off on the Self Check on page 159.*

Lesson 21 **Part 1: Introduction** 👥

Understand Angle Relationships

○ ○ **Where can you find pairs of angles that are congruent?**

You know that vertical angles formed by two intersecting lines have the same measure, so they are congruent. You can also find congruent angles whenever parallel lines are crossed by another line.

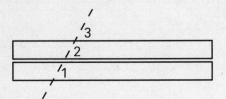

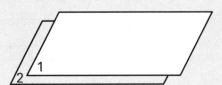

Place parallel strips of paper side by side. Use a ruler to draw a line across them, then cut the strips on the line. Where would you expect two angles to overlap perfectly? Slide one strip to cover the other to check your thinking.

When a third line cuts, or crosses, two lines it is called a **transversal**. When the lines are parallel, the transversal forms pairs of congruent angles called corresponding angles. **Corresponding angles** are angles that are in the same position in the intersections of the transversal and each of the parallel lines. Angles 1, 2, and 3 are above one parallel line and to the right of the transversal, so they are all congruent.

🔍 **Think** You can reason that alternate interior angles are congruent.

You can combine what you know about congruent vertical angles with congruent corresponding angles to find other pairs of congruent angles.

Because ∠2 and ∠5 are vertical angles, ∠2 ≅ ∠5. ∠1 ≅ ∠2 because they are corresponding angles, so that also means that ∠1 ≅ ∠5. Angle pairs such as ∠1 and ∠5 are called **alternate interior angles** because they are inside (between) the two parallel lines and they are on alternate (opposite) sides of the transversal. Alternate interior angles are congruent if created by parallel lines.

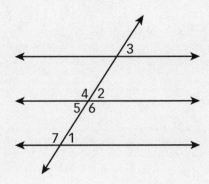

🔍 Think You can reason that same-side interior angles are supplementary.

Adjacent supplementary angles, such as ∠2 and ∠6 are called a **linear pair** because they form a line. Another linear pair is ∠5 and ∠6. The sum of the measures of linear pairs is always 180°.

Combine this with facts about alternate interior angles to learn about **same-side interior angles,** or angles on the same side of a transversal through parallel lines. Since $m\angle 2 + m\angle 6 = 180°$, and since $\angle 1 \cong \angle 2$, then $m\angle 1 + m\angle 6 = 180°$. To use mathematical language, you can say same-side interior angles are supplementary.

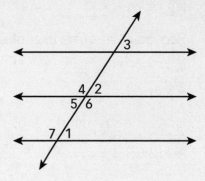

Here are more angle relationships shown in this figure.

∠2 and ∠5 are vertical angles	$\angle 2 \cong \angle 5$
∠1 and ∠2 are corresponding angles	$\angle 1 \cong \angle 2$
∠1 and ∠5 are alternate interior angles	$\angle 1 \cong \angle 5$
∠5 and ∠6 are a linear pair	$m\angle 5 + m\angle 6 = 180°$

✏️ Reflect

1 Name other pairs of corresponding angles, alternate interior angles, vertical angles, and angles in a linear pair.

_____

_____

_____

🔍 Explore It

Recognize vertical angles to find each measure.

2 $m \angle a =$ _____

3 $m \angle b =$ _____

Recognize alternate interior angles to find each measure.

4 $m \angle c =$ _____

5 $m \angle d =$ _____

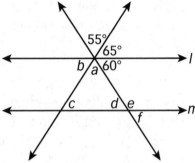

Lines *l* and *m* are parallel.

Use same-side interior angles to find the measure.

6 $m \angle e =$ _____ What is another way to find $m \angle e$?

_____

Use corresponding angles to find the measure.

7 $m \angle f =$ _____ What is another way to find $m \angle f$?

_____

Now try this problem.

8 Lines *p* and *q* are parallel. Give three ways to reason that $\angle 1$ and $\angle 7$ are congruent.

_____

_____

_____

_____

_____

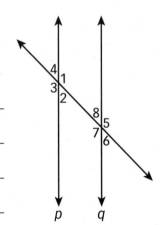

💬 Talk About It

9 In the diagram, *ABCD* is a parallelogram. List all the angles that are congruent to ∠1 and all the angles that are congruent to ∠8. For four of the congruent angles in each set, tell how you know.

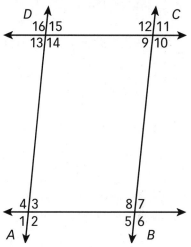

Congruent to ∠1: _____

∠___ reason: _____

∠___ reason: _____

∠___ reason: _____

∠___ reason: _____

_____

Congruent to ∠8: _____

∠___ reason: _____

∠___ reason: _____

∠___ reason: _____

∠___ reason: _____

_____

10 Reasoning about transversals and congruent angles can give you information about different polygons. In the parallelogram formed by these lines, what do you notice about diagonally opposite angles? _____

✏️ Try It Another Way

11 Adam sketches plans for a small wooden table. This side view shows the two legs on one side of the table. Why can you represent the table top and the floor with parallel lines?

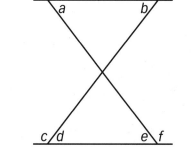

_____

12 Which two pairs of angles are alternate interior angles?

_____

13 If Adam builds the table and doesn't make those angles equal, what will be wrong with his table?

_____

Connect It

Talk through these problems as a class, then write your answers below.

14 Conclude: The diagram shows lines *l, m, n, p,* and *q* all cut by transversal *t.* Which two lines are parallel? How do you know?

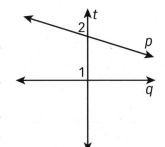

_____

_____

_____

_____

15 Critique: Ari drew the two lines *p* and *q,* and a transversal line *t* perpendicular to *q* with $m\angle 1 = 90°$. He says that since $\angle 1$ and $\angle 2$ are corresponding angles, $\angle 1$ is congruent to $\angle 2$ and $m\angle 2 = 90°$. But when he measures $\angle 2$, he finds that it is 75°. Explain Ari's mistake.

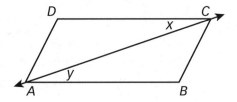

_____

_____

_____

_____

16 Argue: In the diagram, *ABCD* is a parallelogram. Write an argument to support the claim that $m\angle x = m\angle y$.

_____

_____

_____

_____

_____

Put It Together

17 Use what you have learned to complete this task.

> Emily is planning a quilt. She has cut fabric into identical triangles like the ones shown below. She plans to use these triangles to make a border across the top of the quilt.

Show how she can transform the triangles to form a row of triangular pieces to fit between the parallel lines of the border.

A For the first arrangement, begin with the piece shown below.

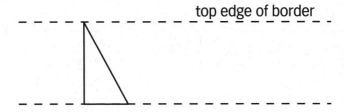

B Show another arrangement, beginning with the piece shown here.

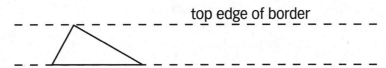

C Emily decides on the arrangement shown below by continuing to transform the triangle. The edges of the border are parallel. Name three pairs of congruent angles. Use angle relationships to explain why they are congruent. Identify a set of supplementary angles.

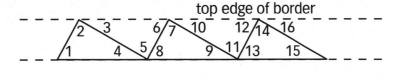

_____

_____

_____

_____

_____

_____

Lesson 22   Part 1: Introduction 👥

Understand Angle Relationships in Triangles

What special angle relationships are in triangles?

You have seen that angles formed by parallel lines and a transversal have important relationships. Angles in triangles also have similar relationships.

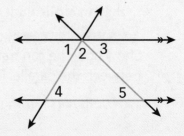

Later in this lesson you will show that the sum of the three angles in any triangle is 180°.

You can use this angle relationship to help you solve problems about triangles and other polygons. For example, you could find the measure of each angle in an equilateral triangle.

🔍 **Think**   The measure of an exterior angle of a triangle plus the measure of the adjacent interior angle = 180°.

An **exterior angle** is the angle formed by extending one side past a vertex.

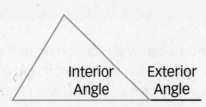

Interior Angle   Exterior Angle

In the diagram below, $m\angle w + m\angle x = 180°$. Why?

The fact that the sum of the three interior angles is also 180° will help you find a relationship between the exterior angle and the other interior angles. You will reason that, in any triangle, the measure of an exterior angle (such as *w*) equals the sum of the two non-adjacent interior angles (*y* and *z*).

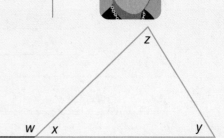

🔍 **Think**
If two angles in one triangle are congruent to two angles in another triangle, then the third angle in each must also be congruent to the other.

> **Mark the congruent angles in the triangles in different colors.**

In the diagram to the right, $\angle B \cong \angle D$ and $\angle A \cong \angle F$.

$20° + 115° + m\angle C = 180°$

$m\angle C = 180° - 135°$

$m\angle C = 45°$

$20° + 115° + m\angle E = 180°$

$m\angle E = 180° - 135°$

$m\angle E = 45°$

So $\angle C \cong \angle E$.

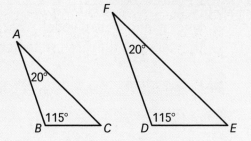

When all three angles are congruent to three angles in another triangle, the two triangles are similar, which means that pairs of corresponding sides are proportional. The triangles above are similar, and $\dfrac{AB}{FD} = \dfrac{BC}{DE} = \dfrac{CA}{EF}$.

✏️ **Reflect**

1. In triangle *PQR*, $m\angle P = 30°$ and $m\angle Q = 60°$. In triangle *STU*, $m\angle S = 30°$ and $m\angle T = 60°$. How do you know that $m\angle R = m\angle U$? How can you prove this using the fact that the angles in a triangle have a sum of 180°?

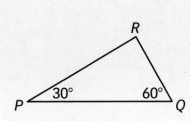 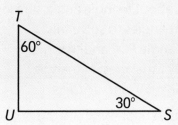

_____

_____

_____

Explore It

2 Explain how you know that $m\angle 1 + m\angle 2 + m\angle 3 = 180°$.

_____

_____

Lines m and n are parallel. What is the relationship that tells you that each statement is true?

3 $m\angle 1 = m\angle 4$ _____

4 $m\angle 3 = m\angle 5$ _____

5 Explain how you can use congruent angles from problems 3 and 4 with the equation in Problem 2 to show that the sum of the angles inside the triangle is 180°.

_____

_____

_____

Now try this problem.

6 Use the fact about triangle angle sums and similar triangles to solve this problem. Triangle *PQR* and triangle *STU* are similar triangles. In triangle *PQR*, $m\angle QPR = 60°$ and $\angle PQR$ is a right angle.

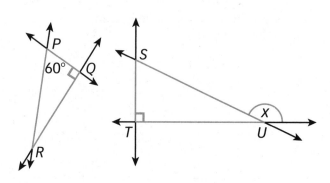

Explain how you can solve for *x*.

_____

_____

_____

Talk About It

You demonstrated on the previous page that the sum of the angles in any triangle is 180°. Now consider these two triangles: $\angle a \cong \angle d$ and $\angle b \cong \angle e$. Complete the reasoning to show that the third pair of angles must also be congruent.

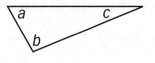
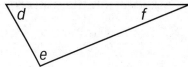

7 How do you know that $c = 180 - a - b$ and $f = 180 - d - e$?

_____

_____

8 Remember that $a = d$ and $b = e$. Why can you say that $c = 180 - d - e$?

_____

9 Remember that $f = 180 - d - e$. Why can you say that $c = f$?

_____

10 Would this reasoning still be true if the triangles were right triangles or isosceles triangles? Explain.

_____

_____

Try It Another Way

11 Draw $\triangle RST$ similar to $\triangle ABC$ using a scale factor of $\frac{1}{2}$. Use a protractor to check that corresponding angles are congruent.

12 Write the proportions you would use to confirm that the two triangles are similar to each other. Measure with a ruler to write the ratios and check to see if they are equal.

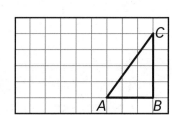

_____

Connect It

Talk through these problems as a class, then write your answers below.

13 Prove: Complete the logic to show that the sum of the two non-adjacent interior angles *y* and *z* equals the measure of the exterior angle *w*.

- Complete the two equations to show the angle relationships you know.

  $x + y + z =$ _____

  $w + x =$ _____

- Solve the first equation for the sum $y + z$ and solve for the second equation for *w*.

  $y + z =$ _____

  $w =$ _____

- How do you know that exterior angle *w* equals the sum of the two non-adjacent interior angles *y* and *z*?

  _____

  _____

14 Explain: In the diagram, $\angle ABC \cong \angle DEC$. Explain how you know that triangle *ABC* and triangle *DEC* are similar triangles.

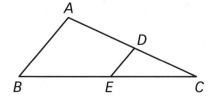

  _____

  _____

  _____

15 Apply: This diagram shows the same similar triangles as in Problem 14. Each segment except $\overline{AB}$ is a road. Between points *A* and *B* is a pond. Explain how you can find the distance across the pond by measuring other distances.

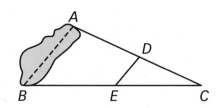

  _____

  _____

🔍 **Put It Together**

16 Use similar triangles to explain why the slope *m* is the same between any two distinct points on the line shown below.

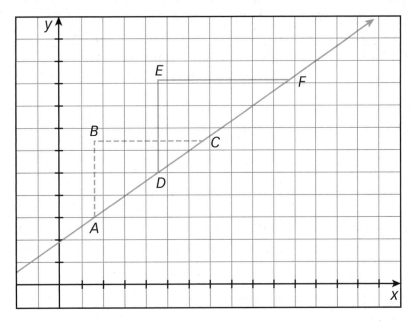

A Use the fact that $\overline{AB}$ is parallel to $\overline{DE}$ and $\overline{BC}$ is parallel to $\overline{EF}$ to find two pairs of congruent angles in triangles *ABC* and *DEF*.

_____

_____

B Explain how you can show that triangles *ABC* and *DEF* are similar triangles.

_____

_____

C The slope of the line between *A* and *C* is $\frac{AB}{BC}$. The slope of the line between *D* and *F* is $\frac{DE}{EF}$. Use similar triangles to explain how you know the slope of the line is the same between both pairs of points.

_____

_____

Lesson 23 Part 1: Introduction

Understand the Pythagorean Theorem

What is the Pythagorean Theorem?

A **theorem** is the statement of a mathematical idea that someone has proven to be true. One of the best known theorems in geometry is the **Pythagorean Theorem**. It states:

The square on the hypotenuse of a right triangle has an area equal to the combined areas of the squares on the other two sides.

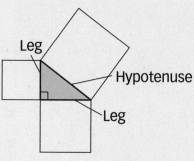

Leg

Hypotenuse

Leg

Another way of stating it is this:

In a right triangle, the sum of the squares of the lengths of the legs is equal to the square of the length of the hypotenuse.

This is often written as $a^2 + b^2 = c^2$, where a, b, and c are the side lengths of the triangle, as shown to the right.

a c

b

In this lesson you will look at different ways this theorem can be proven.

🔍 **Think** You can use a diagram to understand the Pythagorean Theorem.

In this diagram, one side of the right angle (a **leg**) is 3 units long, and one side (a leg) is 4 units long. The squares on those legs are 9 square units and 16 square units. The side opposite the right angle (the **hypotenuse**) is 5 units long. The square on the hypotenuse is 25 square units.

Here, $a^2 + b^2 = c^2$ means $3^2 + 4^2 = 5^2$.

The sum of the squares is 9 + 16, or 25.

> **Shade the hypotenuse of the triangle below with your pencil.**

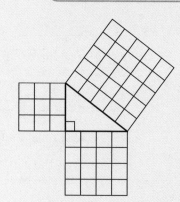

🔍 **Think**   You can use algebra with geometry to prove the Pythagorean Theorem.

To prove that a theorem is true, you need to find a way to show that if a triangle has a 90° angle, no matter what the lengths of the legs (no matter what values *a* and *b* have, even decimals or fractions), the sum of the squares of *a* and *b* equals the square of the length of the hypotenuse.

One way you can do this is by cutting out a right triangle and rearranging copies of it, as shown below. In this lesson, you will show that the area of the white square in Figure 1 has to be the same as the sum of the areas of the two white squares in Figure 2. And you will show that this proves the Pythagorean Theorem.

> *All the triangles in Figure 1 and Figure 2 are right triangles.*

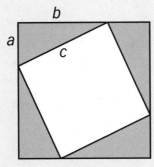

Figure 1

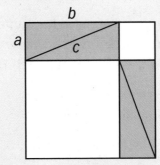

Figure 2

Another proof is based on the lengths of the line segments in Figure 1. You will write expressions to find the areas of the squares, then use those expressions to show that $a^2 + b^2 = c^2$.

✏️ **Reflect**

1 If two legs of a right triangle are 2 inches and 3 inches, can the hypotenuse be 4 inches? Justify your answer.

_____

_____

_____

Explore It

Complete a geometric proof of the Pythagorean Theorem.

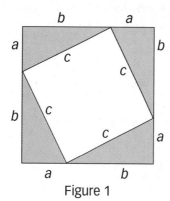

Figure 1

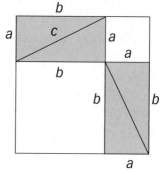

Figure 2

2 Show that the quadrilateral in the center of Figure 1 is a square. Remember, the triangles are right triangles. Use what you know about supplementary angles and the sum of angles in a triangle to show that each angle is 90°. Tell how you know that all sides are congruent.

_____

_____

_____

Similar reasoning shows that both white quadrilaterals in Figure 2 are also squares. Now write expressions for the areas of the three squares.

3 What is the area of the white square in Figure 1? _____ The smaller square in Figure 2 at the top right? _____ The larger square in Figure 2 at the bottom left? _____

Now complete the proof.

4 Justify the statement that the area of the two white squares in Figure 2 together is the same as the area of the white square in Figure 1.

_____

_____

5 How does this prove the Pythagorean Theorem?

_____

_____

Talk About It

Complete an algebraic proof of the Pythagorean Theorem.

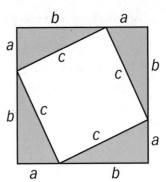

6 The diagram shows four congruent triangles. Write an expression for each area.

one triangle: $A =$ _____

all four triangles: $A =$ _____

the white square: $A =$ _____

the large square with sides $a + b$: $A =$ _____

7 Now write an expression for the area of a square with side lengths $(b + a)$. $A =$ _____

8 Use the distributive property twice to expand $(b + a) \cdot (b + a)$:
$A = (b + a) \cdot \boxed{} + (b + a) \cdot \boxed{}$

9 Then use the distributive property again for each term and simplify:
$A = (b \cdot \boxed{} + a \cdot \boxed{}) + (b \cdot \boxed{} + a \cdot \boxed{})$

$A = \boxed{} + ab + ab + \boxed{}$

$A = \boxed{} + 2ab + \boxed{}$

10 What reasoning allows you to now write that $c^2 + 2ab = b^2 + 2ab + a^2$?

_____

11 Subtract $2ab$ from both sides of the equation in problem 10. What is the result? How does this prove the Pythagorean Theorem?

_____

_____

Try It Another Way

12 Compare the geometric proof on the previous page and the algebraic proof above.

_____

_____

_____

_____

_____

Connect It

Talk through these problems as a class, then write your answers below.

13 Apply: Sketch a right triangle with leg lengths f and g, and hypotenuse h. Write an equation relating f, g, and h. Now use what you know about squares and square roots to write an expression for the length of the hypotenuse, h. Then choose values for f and g, and find an approximate value for h.

_____

_____

_____

_____

14 Generalize: You know a right triangle with legs 3 and 4 units has a hypotenuse of 5 units. Use algebra to show that any right triangle with sides $3n$ and $4n$ has a hypotenuse of $5n$.

_____

_____

_____

_____

15 Analyze: A right triangle with side lengths 5 and 12 has a hypotenuse of length 13. Use arguments based on similar triangles to show that a triangle with sides $5n$, $12n$, and $13n$ is also a right triangle.

_____

_____

_____

_____

Put It Together

16 Prove the reverse (converse) of the Pythagorean Theorem:

If a triangle has sides such that $a^2 + b^2 = c^2$, then it is a right triangle.

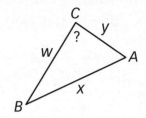

A Start with triangle ABC, where it is given that $x^2 = w^2 + y^2$, but the angles are unknown. Follow the logic below to prove that angle C must be a right angle and triangle ABC must be a right triangle.

  i Sketch a different triangle DEF with a right angle at F, $\overline{FE} = w$ and $\overline{FD} = y$.

  ii How can you find the length of the hypotenuse, $\overline{DE}$?

  _____

  _____

  iii Explain how you know that ABC and DEF are similar triangles.

  _____

  _____

  iv Explain how you know that angle C is a right angle.

  _____

B Summarize the reasoning used above to prove that if a triangle has sides such that $a^2 + b^2 = c^2$, then it is a right triangle.

_____

_____

_____

_____

_____

Lesson 24   Part 1: Introduction 👥

Solve Problems Using the Pythagorean Theorem

You know the relationship between the hypotenuse and the legs of a right triangle. Take a look at this problem.

Ms. Berkin is dividing her $4\frac{1}{2}$-foot by 6-foot bulletin board into 4 sections with ribbon stretched from each corner to the opposite corner. How much yarn does she need?

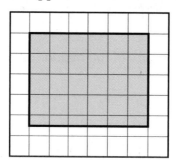

🔍 Explore It

Use math you already know to solve the problem.

- Write the equation for the Pythagorean Theorem for your reference. _____

- In the rectangle, sketch the position of the ribbons and outline a right triangle with a diagonal of the rectangle as the hypotenuse.

- Label the vertical leg *a* and write its length. $a =$ _____

- Label the horizontal leg *b* and write its length. $b =$ _____

- Write an expression for the hypotenuse. $c =$ _____ or _____

- Solve for *c*. $c =$ _____

- How many feet of ribbon does Ms. Berkin need? _____

Find Out More

The Pythagorean Theorem allows you to find an unknown side length in a right triangle by applying the equation $a^2 + b^2 = c^2$. In this equation, a and b are the lengths of the sides adjacent to the right angle (the legs) and c is the length of the side opposite the right angle (the hypotenuse).

The sides a and b of a right triangle may be any length, but often c turns out to be an irrational number, like $\sqrt{13}$. It's helpful to recognize a few sets of side lengths that are whole numbers. These lengths are known as Pythagorean triples.

What are some Pythagorean triples based on multiples of the side lengths of a triangle with sides 3, 4, and 5?

A few Pythagorean triples are listed here. Any whole-number multiple of these side lengths is also a Pythagorean triple.

| 3, 4, 5 | 5, 12, 13 | 8, 15, 17 |

| 7, 24, 25 | 20, 21, 29 |

The Pythagorean Theorem is a powerful tool for finding lengths that are not easily measured, such as the distance across a pond. It is also often used to find lengths in geometric figures that are not right triangles but can be decomposed into right triangles. And it can even be used to find lengths in three-dimensional figures, as in the rectangular prism shown here.

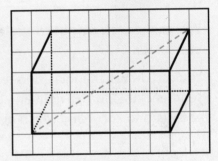

Reflect

1 Is the measure of the hypotenuse of a right triangle with legs that measure 4 and 5 cm a rational number or an irrational number? Justify your answer.

_____

_____

_____

_____

Read the problem below. Then explore different ways to represent and solve problems using the Pythagorean Theorem.

The transmitter for John's thermometer has to be less than 50 feet from the receiver. He places the transmitter, *T*, and the receiver, *R*, at the locations shown. Are the two components less than 50 feet from each other?

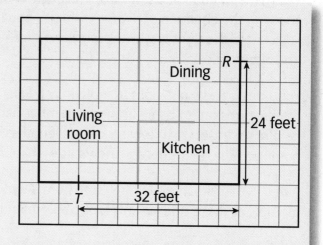

🔍 Picture It

You can sketch a right triangle and label the lengths you know.

You can draw a triangle using two perpendicular line segments that form a right angle. Identify which distance you need to know and which distances you already know.

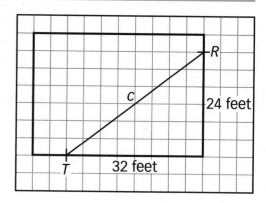

🔍 Model It

You can use an equation to represent the distance.

You have a right triangle, so use the Pythagorean Theorem.

$a^2 + b^2 = c^2$

$24^2 + 32^2 = c^2$

Connect It

Now you will use equations to solve the problem on the previous page.

2 Explain how you know the equation $24^2 + 32^2 = c^2$ represents this situation.

_____

_____

3 Use a calculator to solve for *c* to the nearest foot. Show your work.

_____

4 Are the transmitter and receiver close enough to work?

_____

5 Consider the Pythagorean triples listed in the introduction. Which set of triples does this

problem use? _____

How could you solve the problem using a multiple of that triple instead of using squares
and square roots?

_____

_____

Try It

Use what you just learned about the Pythagorean Theorem to solve this problem.

6 Explain how you might use the Pythagorean Theorem to find the height of this triangle.

_____

_____

_____

_____

_____

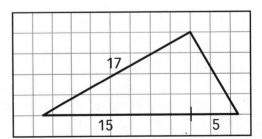

Read the problem below. Then explore different ways to solve problems in three dimensions using the Pythagorean Theorem.

How can you find the length of a diagonal line drawn from point *A* to point *B* in this rectangular prism?

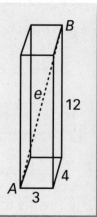

Picture It

You can sketch a diagram to represent the problem.

Look for right triangles that are related to the dimension you want to know.

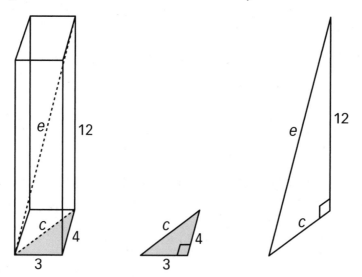

Model It

You can write equations to find the unknown values.

$3^2 + 4^2 = c^2$

$c^2 + 12^2 = e^2$

Connect It

Now you will use the equations on the previous page to solve the problem.

7 In the triangle with sides 3, 4, and *c*, which is the right angle? How do you know?

_____

_____

8 How does finding the length of hypotenuse *c* help you find the length of diagonal *e*?

_____

_____

9 Use the Pythagorean Theorem to find the length of the diagonal *c*. Show your work.

_____

10 Use the Pythagorean Theorem to find the length of the diagonal *e*. Show your work.

_____

11 Explain how to find the length of a diagonal in a right rectangular prism when you know the dimensions of the prism.

_____

_____

12 Explain how you can use substitution to write just one equation for the length *e* when you know *a* and *b*.

_____

Try It

13 Find the length of the diagonal from *P* to *Q*. _____

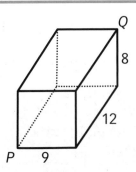

Study the model below. Then solve problems 14–16.

If I can express the height in terms of the width, then I only have one unknown.

Student Model

An older TV screen has a diagonal measurement of 32 inches. The ratio of the width to the height is 4:3. How wide is the screen on a 32-inch TV?

Look at how you could show your work.

$$w^2 + h^2 = d^2$$

$$w^2 + \left(\frac{3}{4}w\right)^2 = 32^2$$

$$\frac{16}{16}w^2 + \frac{9}{16}w^2 = 32^2$$

$$\frac{25}{16}w^2 = 32^2$$

$$\sqrt{\frac{25}{16}w^2} = 32$$

$$\frac{5}{4}w = 32$$

$$w = 25.6$$

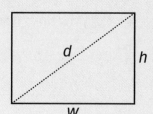

Pair/Share

How would the solution be different if you expressed the width in terms of the height?

Solution: __The screen is 25.6 inches wide.__

This looks like one of those 2-step problems.

14 Mr. Kurdzo wants to store a 12-foot-long pipe in a tool closet that is 6 feet wide, 6 feet long, and 8 feet high. Will it fit?

Show your work.

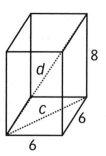

Pair/Share

Can you find two different paths to the solution?

Solution: _____

15 A right triangle has a hypotenuse with a length of 20. The lengths of the legs are whole numbers. What are the lengths of the legs?

Show your work.

I think Pythagorean triples can help me here.

Solution: _____

Pair/Share

How could you use the guess and check strategy on problems like this?

16 Mr. Hill is building a walkway from the corner of his house out to his vegetable garden in the corner of the yard. The dimensions of the yard and the garden are shown. What is the length of the walkway, *w*, to the nearest foot?

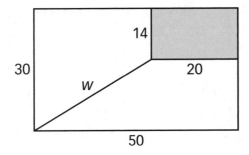

A 25 feet

B 34 feet

C 46 feet

D 58 feet

Where can you draw a useful right triangle?

Adam chose **C** as the correct answer. How did he get that answer?

_____

_____

Pair/Share

Was there more than one helpful right triangle that would lead to the solution?

Solve the problems.

1 What is the best approximation for the length of *GP*?

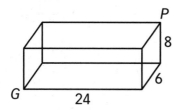

A 22

B 26

C 28

D 38

2 What is the height of the square pyramid?

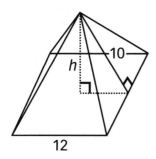

A 4

B 8

C 12

D 16

3 In right triangle *ABC*, side *BC* is longer than side *AB*. The boxed numbers represent the possible side lengths of triangle *ABC*.

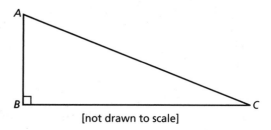

| 7 | 8 | 9 | 10 |

| 24 | 25 | 26 | 27 |

A

B ⌐

C

[not drawn to scale]

Identify three boxed numbers that could be the side lengths of triangle *ABC*. Enter the number you chose to represent the length of each side.

AB = ☐

BC = ☐

CA = ☐

4 Two sides of a right triangle have lengths of 26 units and 10 units. There are two possible lengths for the third side.

What is the shortest possible side length? ☐ units

What is the longest possible side length? ☐ units

5 A car salesman is stringing banners from the top of the roof to a fence pole 20 feet away. The top of the roof is 29 feet from the ground. The fence pole is 8 feet high. How many feet of banner rope does he need to reach from the rooftop to the fence pole?

Show your work.

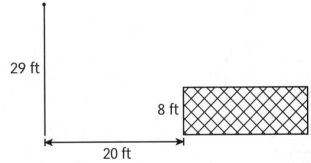

Answer _____

6 What are the dimensions of the largest square with whole-number side lengths that can fit into a circle with a radius of 5 units?

Show your work.

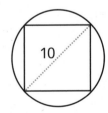

Answer _____

✓ **Self Check** *Go back and see what you can check off on the Self Check on page 159.*

Lesson 25   Part 1: Introduction 👥

Distance in the Coordinate Plane

You have solved problems with two- and three-dimensional figures using the Pythagorean Theorem. Take a look at this problem.

What is the distance between (2, 3) and (5, 7) in the coordinate plane?

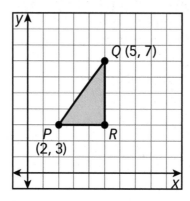

🔍 Explore It

Use math you already know to solve the problem.

▪ Write the equation for the Pythagorean Theorem for your reference. _____

▪ How do you know triangle *PQR* is a right triangle?

_____

▪ Label the legs of triangle *PQR* *a* and *b* and label the hypotenuse *c*.

▪ What is the distance from point *P* to point *R*? _____

▪ What is the distance from point *Q* to point *R*? _____

▪ Write a numerical expression for the length of the hypotenuse, *c*. _____

▪ Explain how you can find the distance between points *P* and *Q*.

_____

🔍 Find Out More

The Pythagorean Theorem gives you the tools to find the distance between any two given points in the coordinate plane.

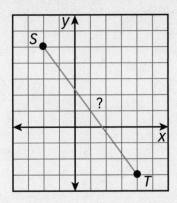

Pythagorean triples can come in handy in the coordinate plane, too.

If you know the coordinates of any two points you can find the distance between them. Draw a vertical line through one point and a horizontal line through the other point to create a right triangle.

Find the distance from each point to the vertex of the right angle. Then use those distances as the lengths of the legs. Use the equation for the Pythagorean Theorem to find an expression for the length of the hypotenuse. That is the distance between the two given points.

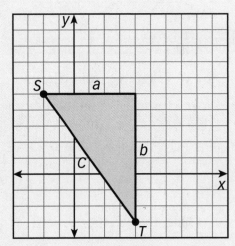

✏️ Reflect

1 Describe how finding the distance between two points in the coordinate plane is similar to finding the hypotenuse of a triangle.

_____

_____

_____

Read the problem below. Then explore different ways to find the distance between two points in the coordinate plane.

What is the distance between the points (−5, −3) and (−2, 4)?

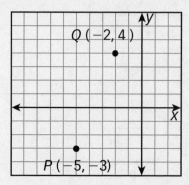

Picture It

You can sketch a right triangle.

Draw a vertical line segment from one point and a horizontal line segment from the other. *PQR* is a right triangle. *PR* and *QR* are legs. *PQ* is the hypotenuse.

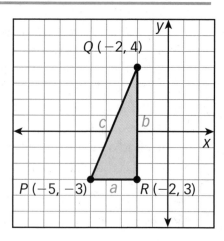

Model It

You can use equations to represent the lengths of the legs.

$a = |-2 - (-5)|$

$b = |4 - (-3)|$

$c^2 = a^2 + b^2$

Connect It

Now you will use equations to solve the problem.

2 Explain how you know the equation $PR^2 + QR^2 = PQ^2$ is true for triangle PQR on the previous page.

_____

_____

_____

3 What is the length of a? _____

4 What is the length of b? _____

5 What is the length of c? _____

6 What is the distance between $(-5, -3)$ and $(-2, 4)$? _____

7 Explain how to find the distance between any two points in the coordinate plane.

_____

_____

_____

Try It

Use what you just learned to solve these problems. Show your work on a separate sheet of paper.

8 Find the distance between points J and K. _____

9 Find the distance between points K and L. _____

10 Classify triangle JKL and justify your answer.

_____

_____

_____

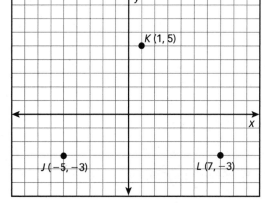

Study the model below. Then solve problems 11–13.

I guess I need to use the Pythagorean Theorem two times.

Classify the triangle formed by points (–1, 2), (1, –1) and (–2, –1) as scalene, isosceles, or equilateral. Justify your answer.

Look at how you could show your work.

$$AB = \sqrt{1^2 + 3^2} = \sqrt{10}$$

$$BC = \sqrt{2^2 + 3^2} = \sqrt{13}$$

$$AC = 3$$

$$\sqrt{10} \neq \sqrt{13} \neq 3$$

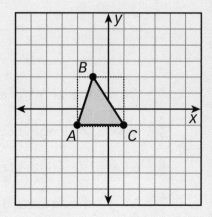

⬤ **Pair/Share**

Why did the student not find exact values for the side lengths?

Solution: _The triangle is scalene; all three sides have different lengths._

Where's the right triangle?

11 Find the distance between the points (3, –2) and (–5, 4).

Show your work.

_____

_____

_____

_____

_____

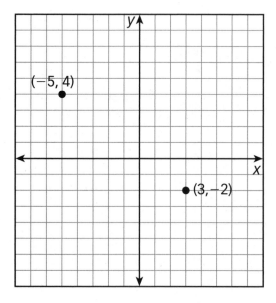

⬤ **Pair/Share**

What other ways can you find the solution?

Solution: _____

12 Draw a line segment from the origin (0, 0) with length $\sqrt{10}$.

Show your work.

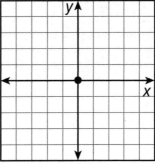

Hmm. I need a right triangle with hypotenuse $\sqrt{10}$.

◯Pair/Share

How many different solutions to this problem can you find?

Solution: _____

13 Which expression can be used to find the distance between points (−1, −1) and (19, 20)?

A　$AB = \sqrt{2^2 + 4^2} = \sqrt{20}$

B　$d = \sqrt{(19 - 1)^2 + (20 - 1)^2}$

C　$d = \sqrt{(-1 - 1)^2 + (20 - 19)^2}$

D　$d = \sqrt{(19 + 1)^2 + (20 + 1)^2}$

Adam chose **B** as the correct answer. How did he get that answer?

_____

_____

_____

_____

How does this relate to a right triangle?

◯Pair/Share

If you check your answer with a calculator does it seem reasonable?

Solve the problems.

1 Segment *AB* begins at *A*(2, 1) and ends at point *B*(6, 4). The segment is dilated by a factor of 2 with the center of dilation at the origin to form segment *A'B'*. Segment *A'B'* is then translated 4 units left and 2 units down to form segment *A''B''*. Choose True or False for each statement.

A Segment *A''B''* is congruent to segment *AB*. ☐ True ☐ False

B The coordinates of *A''* are those of the origin. ☐ True ☐ False

C The distance between *A* and *B* is one half the distance between *A'* and *B'*. ☐ True ☐ False

D Segment *A''B''* has the same length as segment *A'B'*. ☐ True ☐ False

E The length of *A''B''* would be different if the translation had occurred before the dilation. ☐ True ☐ False

2 Decide which of the following points, *A* through *G*, belong in each of the three categories in the table. Then write the letter of the point in the proper column.

A (−7, −5) *B* (14, −4) *C* (6, 8) *D* (2, 8) *E* (9, 9) *F* (6, −8)	A point greater than 10 units from the origin	A point exactly 10 units from the origin	A point less than 10 units from the origin

3 Find the perimeter of parallelogram *ABCD* with vertices at (−3, 3), (3, 3), (0, −1), and (−6, −1).

Show your work.

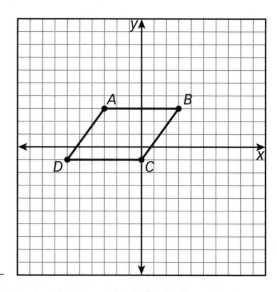

Answer _____

4 Draw the reflection of triangle *ABC* in the *y*-axis. Then show that the corresponding sides of the two triangles are congruent.

Show your work.

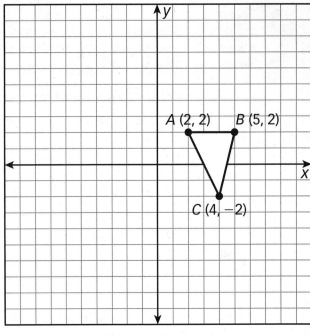

5 Segment *AB* is one side of a square. Find the coordinates of the other two vertices of the square. Explain your reasoning. More than one answer is possible.

_____

_____

_____

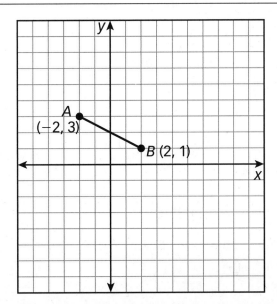

Understand Volume of Cylinders, Cones, and Spheres

How is finding the volume of a cylinder like finding the volume of a rectangular prism?

You already know that the volume of a rectangular prism is equal to the area of the base of the prism times the height.

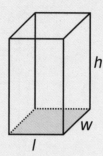

Volume of a rectangular prism = Area of the base • height = (length • width) • height

You can find the volume of a cylinder in the same way.

Think   How can you find the volume of a cylinder?

The volume of a cylinder can be found by multiplying the area of the base of the cylinder by the height. But in the case of the cylinder, the base is a circle, not a rectangle.

> **Circle the information you use to find the area of the base of the cylinder.**

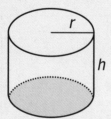

Use the formula for the area of a circle to find the area of the base of the cylinder. The radius of the cylinder is r, so the area of the base is πr^2.

Now we can find the volume of the cylinder.

Volume of a cylinder = Area of the base • height
$$= (\pi r^2) \cdot h$$
$$= \pi r^2 h$$

Think What are the formulas for the volume of a cone and the volume of a sphere?

The cone and the half sphere below are both shown inside a cylinder. The cylinders, the cone, and the half sphere all have the same circle as their base. They all have the same height, too.

How many half spheres make a whole sphere?

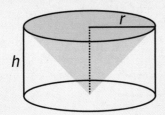 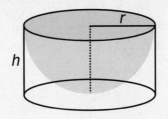

The volume of the cone is $\frac{1}{3}$ the volume of the cylinder.

The volume of the half sphere is $\frac{2}{3}$ the volume of the cylinder.

You can use these relationships to determine the formula for the volume of a cone and the formula for the volume of a sphere.

Volume of Cone

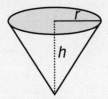

$$\text{Volume} = \frac{1}{3} \cdot \text{area of the base} \cdot \text{height}$$

$$= \frac{1}{3} \cdot \text{area of a circle} \cdot \text{height}$$

$$= \frac{1}{3} \pi r^2 h \text{ or } \frac{\pi r^2 h}{3}$$

Volume of Sphere

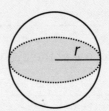

$$\text{Volume} = 2 \cdot \text{volume of half sphere}$$

$$= 2 \cdot \frac{2}{3} \cdot \text{area of the base} \cdot \text{height}$$

$$= \frac{4}{3} \cdot \pi r^2 \cdot r$$

$$= \frac{4}{3} \pi r^3$$

Reflect

1 How can you use the formula for the volume of a cylinder to remember the formulas for the volume of a cone and the volume of a sphere?

_____

_____

_____

🔍 Explore It

You can compare the volumes of cylinders and cones. Use the pictures below to answer problems 2–8.

2

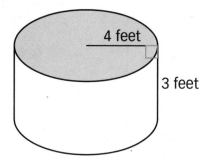
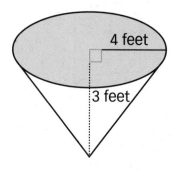

3   How is the base of the cylinder related to the base of the cone?

_____

4   How are the heights of the cylinder and the cone related?

_____

5   Find the volume of the cylinder. Write your answer in terms of π.

_____

6   Find the volume of the cone. Write your answer in terms of π.

_____

7   How does the volume of the cylinder compare to the volume of the cone?

_____

8   Suppose you fill the cone with water and empty the water into the cylinder. How many times will you empty the water from the cone into the cylinder? Explain.

_____

_____

_____

Talk About It

Solve the problems below as a group.

9 The formula for the volume of a cylinder is $V = \pi r^2 h$. The formula can also be written $V = Bh$. What does B represent? _____

_____

10 Complete the equation below using your answers to problems 4 and 5 on the previous page.

Volume of the cone • _____ = Volume of the cylinder

11 Explain how you can use the equation in problem 8 to write a formula for the volume of any cone using B to represent the area of the base of the cone.

_____

_____

_____

12 Compare the volume formulas for spheres and cylinders. Why do you find r^3 to find the volume of a sphere when you only find r^2 to find the volume of a cylinder?

_____

_____

_____

_____

Try Another Problem

13 If the radius of a cylinder is doubled, will the volume be doubled? Explain.

_____

_____

_____

Connect It

Talk through these problems as a class and write your answers below.

14 **Compare:** The water glasses below are filled to the same height and have the same radius. How many times could you fill Glass B to equal the amount water in Glass A? Explain your reasoning.

Glass A   Glass B

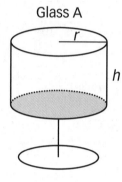 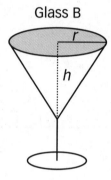

_____

_____

_____

15 **Analyze:** If the radius of a sphere is doubled, how does the volume change? Support your answer by finding the volume of a sphere with $r = 2a$ and comparing it to the volume of a sphere with $r = a$.

_____

_____

16 **Explain:** Explain what πr^2 and h represent in terms of the cylinder. Then explain how this information is used to find the formula for the volume of a half sphere, $\frac{2}{3} \cdot \pi r^2 \cdot r$. Then explain how you use this formula to get the formula $\frac{4}{3} \pi r^3$ for the volume of a sphere.

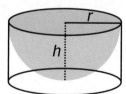

🔍 **Put It All Together**

17 Use what you have learned to answer the questions below.

A Describe the relationship between the volumes of the solids. Which solid has the greatest volume? Which solid has the second greatest volume? Do any of the solids have the same volumes? Explain your reasoning. (Represent volumes in terms of π.)

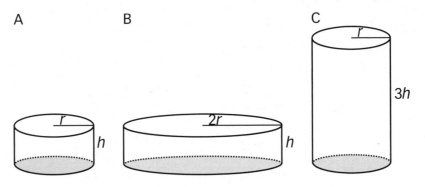

_____

_____

_____

B Describe the relationship between the volumes of the solids. Which solid has the greatest volume? Which solid has the second greatest volume? Do any of the solids have the same volumes? Explain your reasoning. (Represent any volumes in terms of π.

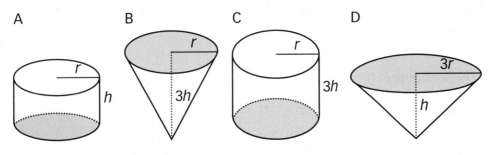

_____

_____

_____

_____

Lesson 27   Part 1: Introduction

Solve Problems with Cylinders, Cones, and Spheres

CCSS
8.G.C.9

In Lesson 26, you learned about the formulas for the volumes of cylinders, cones, and spheres. In this lesson, you will use these formulas to solve problems.

Janet is making homemade candles. She has two candle molds, a prism and a cylinder. Which mold uses the least amount of wax?

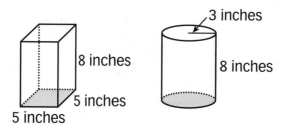

🔍 Explore It

● Explain how to use the area of the base to find the volume of the prism.

_____

● What is the volume of wax needed for the candle in the shape of a prism?

_____

● Explain how to find the volume of a cylinder.

_____

● What is the shape of the base of the cylinder? _____

● What is the area of the base of the cylinder in terms of π? _____

● Write an expression for the volume of the cylinder in terms of π. _____

● What is the volume of the cylinder? (Use 3.14 for π and round your answer to the nearest tenth.) _____

● Which candle uses the least amount of wax? Explain.

_____

_____

🔍 Find Out More

The formula for the volume of a cylinder is related to the formula for the volume of a prism. In both cases, you multiply the area of the base times the height.

The formula for the volume of a cylinder can be used to remember the formula for the volume of a cone with the same radius and height and the volume of a sphere with the same radius. The volume of a cone is $\frac{1}{3}$ the volume of the cylinder and the volume of the sphere is $\frac{4}{3}$ the volume of the cylinder.

Volume of a cylinder = Area of the base · height

$$= (\pi r^2) \cdot h$$

$$= \pi r^2 h$$

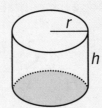

Volume of a cone = $\frac{1}{3}$ · area of the base · height

$$= \frac{1}{3} \cdot \pi r^2 h$$

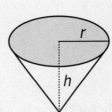

Volume of a sphere = $\frac{4}{3} \cdot \pi r^2 \cdot r$

$$= \frac{4}{3} \pi r^3$$

The "height" of a half-sphere is another radius, so $h = r$.

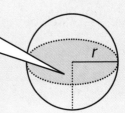

✏️ Reflect

1 How can you use the formula for the volume of a prism to remember the formula for the volume of a cylinder? How is the formula for the volume of a cone related to the formula for the volume of a cylinder?

_____

_____

_____

_____

Read the problem below. Then explore how to find the volume of each figure.

Mark is buying a container to plant flowers in. His choices are a container in the shape of a cone with a height of 24 inches and a radius of 6 inches or one in the shape of a cylinder with a height of 8 inches and a diameter of 12 inches. Which container holds the least amount of soil?

Picture It

Make a sketch for each container.

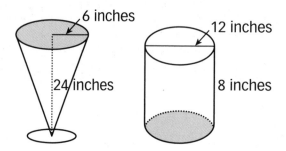

Model It

Use the formula for the volume of a cone.

Volume of a cone $= \frac{1}{3}$ • area of the base • height

$$= \frac{1}{3} \pi r^2 h$$

$$= \frac{1}{3} \pi \cdot (6)^2 \cdot 24$$

Model It

Use the formula for the volume of a cylinder.

Volume of a cylinder $=$ area of the base • height

$$= \pi r^2 h$$

$$= \pi \cdot (6)^2 \cdot 8$$

Connect It

Now you will compare the volumes of the containers on the previous page.

2 How does the radius of the cone compare to the radius of the cylinder?

_____

3 How does the height of the cone compare to the height of the cylinder?

_____

4 How does the formula for the volume of a cone compare to the formula for the volume of a cylinder?

_____

5 Based on your answers to problems 2, 3, and 4, what do you think will be the ratio of the volume of the cone to the volume of the cylinder? Explain your reasoning.

_____

_____

_____

6 Find the volume of each container. Write the volume in terms of π.

cone = _____ cylinder = _____

7 Which container holds the least amount of soil?

_____

Try It

Use what you just learned about volume to solve these problems.

8 What is the volume of wax in the candle shaped like a cylinder? Use 3.14 for π and round your answer to the nearest tenth.

_____

9 What is the volume of wax in the candle shaped like a cone? Use 3.14 for π and round your answer to the nearest tenth.

_____

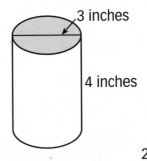

3 inches

4 inches

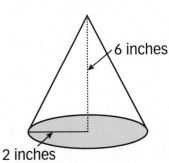

6 inches

2 inches

Read the problem below. Then explore how to find the volume of each figure.

A florist offers vases in three different sizes. Which vase holds the most water?

Height: 20 cm
Diameter: 10 cm

Height: 30 cm
Diameter: 10 cm

Diameter: 10 cm

Model It

Use the formula for the volume of a cylinder.

Volume of a cylinder $= \pi r^2 h$

$\qquad\qquad\qquad = \pi \cdot (5)^2 \cdot 20$

Model It

Use the formula for the volume of a cone.

Volume of a cone $= \frac{1}{3} \cdot \pi r^2 h$

$\qquad\qquad\qquad = \frac{1}{3} \pi \cdot (5)^2 \cdot 30$

Model It

Use the formula for the volume of a sphere.

Volume of a sphere $= \frac{4}{3} \pi r^3$

$\qquad\qquad\qquad = \frac{4}{3} \pi \cdot (5)^3$

Connect It

Now you will compare the volumes of the containers on the previous page. Use 3.14 for π and round your answer to the nearest whole number.

10 How much water does the vase in the shape of a cylinder hold? _____

11 How much water does the vase in the shape of a cone hold? _____

12 How much water does the vase in the shape of a sphere hold? _____

13 Which vase holds the most water?

_____

14 The florist buys new vases from a different supplier. The vases are the same shapes and have the same heights, but the diameter of each vase is 1 cm less than the original vases. Find the volume of water each of the new vases will hold.

cylinder = _____ cone = _____ sphere = _____

15 By what percent did the volume of each shape decrease? Round to the nearest whole percent.

cylinder _____ cone _____ sphere _____

16 Look at the exponent of *r* in each of the three volume formulas. Explain why the sphere had the largest percent change in volume.

_____

_____

_____

Try It

Use what you just learned about volume to solve this problem. Round to the nearest whole number.

17 Find the volume of the beach ball and the volume of the toy ball. How many times greater is the volume of the beach ball than the volume of the toy ball?

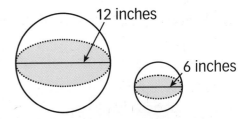

12 inches

6 inches

_____

_____

Study the model below. Then solve problems 18–20.

The radius is half of the diameter, so the student used 3 for the radius of the sphere and 1.5 for the radius of the cylinder.

Student Model

Justin's bird feeder is shown. About how much bird seed, rounded to the nearest whole number, does the bird feeder hold?

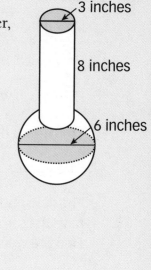

3 inches

8 inches

6 inches

Look at how you could show your work using the formulas for the volumes of cylinders and spheres.

Volume of Sphere

$$V = \frac{4}{3}\pi \cdot (3)^3$$

$$= 36\pi$$

$$36\pi + 18\pi = 54\pi$$

$$\approx 54 \cdot 3.14$$

$$\approx 169.56$$

Volume of Cylinder

$$V = \pi \cdot (1.5)^2 \cdot 8$$

$$= 18\pi$$

Pair/Share

Why do you add the two volumes?

Solution: ___The feeder holds about 170 in.³ of bird seed.___

What is the height of the punch if it is 1 inch less than the height of the punch bowl?

18 A punch bowl is in the shape of a cylinder. The height of the punch bowl is 10 inches and the diameter of the punch bowl is 14 inches. What is the volume of punch you need to fill the punch bowl 1 inch from the top? (Use 3.14 for π and round your answer to the nearest whole.)

Show your work.

Pair/Share

Why doesn't it make sense to find the volume using the height of the entire punch bowl?

Solution: _____

19 The birthday candle shown has a radius of 5 mm. How much wax is needed to make the candle? Use 3.14 for π and round your answer to the nearest whole number.

Show your work.

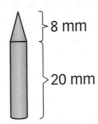

8 mm

20 mm

I think that there are at least three different steps to solve this problem.

🗨**Pair/Share**

How is this problem different from others you've seen in this lesson?

Solution: _____

20 A container for a hanging plant is a half sphere with a diameter of 9 inches. About how much soil does the container hold? Circle the correct answer.

A 191 in.³

B 382 in.³

C 1,526 in.³

D 3,052 in.³

Rob chose **C** as the correct answer. How did he get that answer?

_____

_____

_____

_____

What do you need to do to the formula for the volume of a sphere to find the formula for the volume of a half sphere?

🗨**Pair/Share**

What does Rob need to do with his answer to find the correct answer?

Solve the problems.

1 An automatic dog feeder in the shape of a cone has a height of 18 centimeters. If it holds about 8,308 cubic centimeters of dog food, about what is its radius?

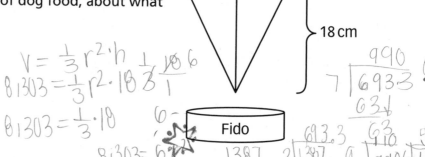

A 7 cm

B 14 cm

C 21 cm

D 49 cm

Handwritten work:
$V = \frac{1}{3}r^2 \cdot h$
$8,303 = \frac{1}{3}r^2 \cdot 18$
$8,303 = \frac{1}{3} \cdot 18$
$8,303 = 6$

Fido

$9 - 2 = 7$

2 A serving bowl has two parts, a half sphere that holds food and a cylinder base that holds cold water to keep the food cold. Which expression represents the volume of water in the cylinder base?

A $\pi r^2 h$

B $\pi r^2 h + \frac{2}{3}\pi r^3$

C $\pi r^2 h - \frac{2}{3}\pi r^3$ (circled)

D $\pi r^2 h - \frac{4}{3}\pi r^3$

Handwritten: subtract b/c you want to find the difference

$\pi r^2 h - \frac{2}{3}\pi r^3$

3 A sphere and a cone have the same volume, and each has a radius of 6 centimeters. What is the height of the cone?

The height of the cone is ⬚ 12 ⬚ cm

Handwritten work:
$V = \frac{1}{3}r^2 \cdot h$
$\frac{1}{3} \cdot 6^2 \cdot h$
$\frac{1}{3} \cdot 36$
$\frac{1}{3} \cdot \frac{36}{1} = \frac{36}{3} \quad 12$
$h = 12$

4 At a construction site, a crane is lifting water in cone-shaped container and transferring the water to a cylindrical storage tank.

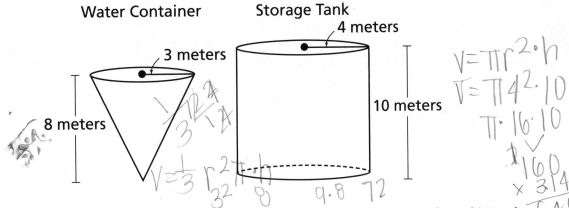

Water Container   Storage Tank

3 meters   4 meters

8 meters   10 meters

$V = \frac{1}{3} r^2 \pi \cdot h$

$V = \pi r^2 \cdot h$
$V = \pi 4^2 \cdot 10$
$\pi \cdot 16 \cdot 10$

160
× 3.14
640
0000
+ 0000
48000
48640

What is the maximum number of full buckets of water that can be transferred into the storage tank without the water overflowing the tank? Shade in the maximum number of buckets possible.

Water Containers

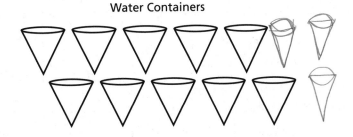

5 Kristen gets a full scoop of frozen yogurt in a cone. The scoop is a perfect sphere that fits just inside the rim of the cone. She wonders if the entire volume of the frozen yogurt could fit completely inside the cone. What is the relationship between the volume of the cone and the volume of frozen yogurt? Is the volume of the cone great enough to fit all of the frozen yogurt? Explain. (Use 3.14 for π and round your answer to the nearest whole number.)

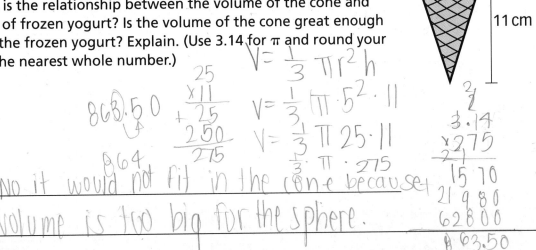

5 cm

11 cm

$V = \frac{1}{3} \pi r^2 h$

$V = \frac{1}{3} \pi \cdot 5^2 \cdot 11$

$V = \frac{1}{3} \pi 25 \cdot 11$

$\frac{1}{3} \cdot \pi \cdot 275$

25
× 11
25
250
275

863.50

864

3.14
× 275
15 70
21 9 80
62800
863.50

No it would not fit in the cone because its volume is too big for the sphere.

✓ **Self Check** *Go back and see what you can check off on the Self Check on page 159.*

Solve the problems.

1 Which sequence of transformations is performed so that Figure 1 is congruent to Figure 2?

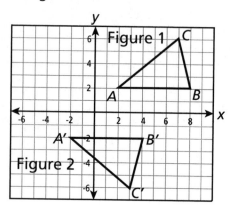

A Figure 1 is reflected over the *x*-axis and translated 4 units to the left.

B Figure 1 is reflected over the *y*-axis and translated 4 units down.

C Figure 1 is rotated 180° counterclockwise around the origin and translated 6 units to the right.

D Figure 1 is rotated 90° clockwise around the origin and translated 6 units down.

2 Which is closest to the amount of water that fills a water balloon with a diameter of 6 inches?

A 904.32 in.³

B 150.72 in.³

C 113.04 in.³

D 63.585 in.³

3 Two right triangles overlap, as shown below.

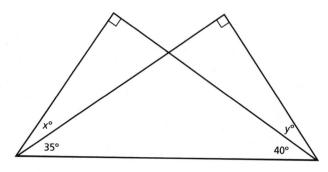

What are the values of *x* and *y*?

$x = \boxed{}$ degrees

$y = \boxed{}$ degrees

4 Marcus needs a right cylindrical storage tank that holds between 150 and 160 cubic feet of water. Using each digit only once, find the radius and height of three different water tanks that hold between 150 and 160 cubic feet of water.

1	2	3	4	5	6	7	8	9

	Radius (feet)	Height (feet)
Tank #1		
Tank #2		
Tank #3		

5   Haley drew triangle *JKL* on the grid below.

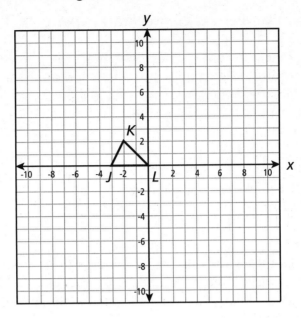

Part A

Draw triangle *MNL* using a scale factor of 3 and the origin as the center.

Part B

If you were to reflect *MNL* over the *x*-axis, what would be the new coordinates of point *M*?

Answer _____

6   In the figure to the right, lines *p* and *q* are parallel.
$m\angle 1 = 67°$, and $m\angle 3 = 63°$. What is $m\angle 4$?
Explain your reasoning.

_____

_____

_____

_____

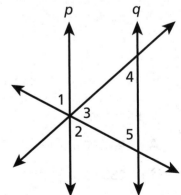

Performance Task

Answer the questions and show all your work on separate paper.

Flix Movies sells mini-popcorn snacks in cone-shaped containers for $2.00 each. Customers have complained that this container is too small, and the owner, Mick, agrees. The container Mick uses has a diameter of 6 centimeters and a height of 14 centimeters. He thinks he should double the volume of the container to hold more popcorn.

Investigate what happens to the volume of the cone when you change the dimensions (try doubling the diameter, or doubling the height, or both.) Show and explain your results each time you change the dimensions.

What is one way Mick could change the dimensions if he wants to triple the volume of the container? Decide if this results in a reasonable container for popcorn and explain why or why not. If you don't think it is a reasonable container, make a suggestion for how he might change the dimensions of the cone to satisfy his customers.

Reflect on Mathematical Practices

After you complete the task, choose one of the following questions to answer.

1. **Reason Mathematically** How does the formula for finding the volume of a cone help explain how the volume changes as you change different dimensions?

2. **Argue and Critique** What criteria did you use to help you decide which size cone Mick should finally use?

©Curriculum Associates, LLC　Copying is not permitted.

If you save your $10 allowance each week and record your growing total savings on a coordinate graph, your graph will be linear. If you ask all of your classmates to measure their heights and weights, and then record this on a coordinate graph, your graph may look sort of like a line. What if you ask your classmates to record their heights and the distances they travel from home to school, then graph this information on a coordinate graph? Will this data be linear or almost linear?

In this unit, you will graph data that is approximately linear and use the equation of a line to answer questions about the data.

✓ Self Check

Before starting this unit, check off the skills you know below. As you complete each lesson, see how many more you can check off!

I can:	Before this unit	After this unit
construct a scatter plot of bivariate data	☐	☐
fit a trend line to a scatter plot	☐	☐
interpret the slope and intercept of trend lines in scatter plots to solve problems	☐	☐
display data in a two-way frequency table	☐	☐
interpret a two-way frequency table to identify possible associations between two categorical variables	☐	☐

Lesson 28   Part 1: Introduction 👥

Scatter Plots

In previous lessons, you learned how to represent relationships between two variables on the coordinate plane. Take a look at this problem.

> Mr. Finley wanted to see if there was a relationship between students' scores on the final exam in algebra and the amount of time they spent studying for it. Students studied for the test by doing practice problems on a website that recorded the minutes they spent studying. He recorded the minutes of studying and test scores in a table. Does the table show a relationship?

🔍 Explore It

Use the math you already know to solve the problem.

Minutes Studied	Test Score
60	85
65	85
70	90
90	100
88	94
99	98
86	38
99	99
96	95
45	70
30	60
56	72
30	35
40	52
25	30

▪ What is the highest score on the exam and the corresponding studying time? _____

▪ What is the lowest score on the exam and the corresponding studying time? _____

▪ What is the approximate mean test score and mean studying time, to the nearest tenth? _____

▪ Are there any ordered pairs that are surprising to you? Explain.

_____

_____

_____

▪ Do you think that spending more time studying helped these students do better on the test? Why or why not?

_____

_____

_____

Find Out More

A **scatter plot** is a graph of ordered pairs in the coordinate plane that represents data. Each ordered pair reports information about two variables. Mr. Finley's data compares minutes a student spent studying (the *x*-coordinate) with that student's test score (the *y*-coordinate). The study of two related variables is called **bivariate data analysis**.

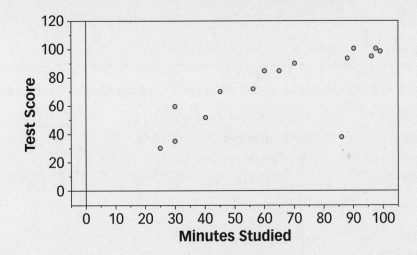

Scatter plots show characteristics of data sets that are not easily seen in tables. For example, notice the clustering above. Points outside the main cluster of data stand out. The ordered pair (86, 38) is outside the main cluster. This point might be considered an **outlier**.

Scatter plots also help reveal the type of **association** there may be between two variables. The test scores and time spent studying show a **positive association** because as time spent studying increased, test scores tended to increase as well. A positive association is represented by an upward trend from left to right in the scatter plot. A **negative association** shows a downward trend from left to right; one variable decreases as the other increases.

In this scatter plot, the trend of the data could be modeled by a straight line through the cluster of points. So, you could describe the relationship shown in the graph as being roughly **linear**. This is not true for all scatter plots. Some may show **non-linear** relationships.

Reflect

1 Is it surprising that there is a positive association between the variables in Mr. Finley's data set rather than a negative association? Why or why not?

_____

_____

_____

Read the problem below. Then explore relationships in bivariate data sets.

> Mr. Finley wondered if there was a relationship between the number of texts students sent the day before the final exam and their test scores. He asked students to volunteer the data from their cell phones, and then he compared it against their test scores. How can he identify trends?

Model It

You can plot the data in a table and scatter plot to show clusters and associations.

Add a horizontal line to represent the mean score and a vertical line to represent the mean number of texts. Look for trends by finding the quadrants that contain large clusters of points.

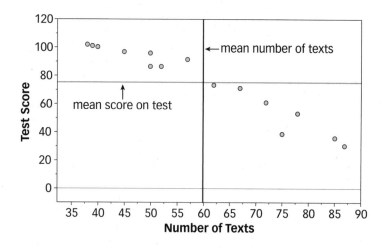

Score on Test	Number of Texts
85	50
85	52
90	57
100	38
94	50
98	40
38	75
99	39
95	45
70	67
60	72
72	62
35	85
52	78
30	67

Model It

You can also cut the scatter plot into vertical slices and compute the mean test score for each slice.

The triangles point to the mean test score for each slice to its right. This representation gives more information about the trend of the data.

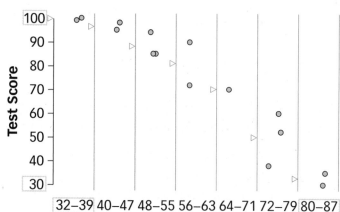

Connect It

Now you will analyze the data set from the previous page.

2 What is the greatest number of text messages sent? What is the least number sent?

_____

3 Are there any points that lie outside the general trend of the data? Explain. You may want to compare the data on the previous page with the scatter plot in the introduction.

_____

_____

4 Does the scatter plot in the first Model It show a positive association or a negative association? Explain. _____

_____

5 How does showing a horizontal line for one mean and a vertical line for the other mean help support your answer to Problem 4?

_____

_____

_____

6 Describe the trend with the means in the sliced scatter plot, which is in the second Model It. How does the trend with the means help support your answer to Problem 4?

_____

_____

_____

Try It

Use what you just learned about associations between variables to solve this problem. Show your work on a separate sheet of either lined paper or graph paper.

7 Describe a situation where a negative association would exist between two variables. Explain why you would expect a negative association. Then make up a data set with 15 ordered pairs and graph them in a scatter plot.

_____

Read the situation described below. Then solve problems 8–10.

You can cut a scatter plot into four parts by making a horizontal line to show the mean y-value and a vertical line for the mean x-value.

Student Model

Mr. Finley's class tried a new website to study for the next test. Mr. Finley again compared time spent studying against test scores using the data displays below.

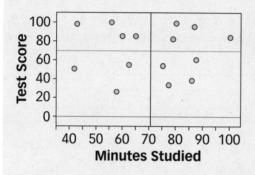

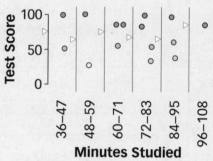

Does there seem to be an association between time spent studying on the new website and test scores?

Possible answer: There is no clear upward or downward trend

in the data displays. Points appear to be randomly scattered

throughout the scatter plot. About the same number of points

fall within each quadrant. The mean for each slice does not

increase or decrease with a consistent trend.

Pair/Share

Name another real-world pair of variables that might have no association with each other.

Scatter plots help us decide what kind of association might exist between two variables.

Pair/Share

Does the first website <u>cause</u> students to get higher test scores? Could other factors not shown by the data set affect test scores?

8 Do you think Mr. Finley should encourage students to study algebra on the website mentioned in the introduction or on this new website?

_____

_____

_____

_____

_____

_____

9 Look at the quadrants in the graph on the previous page. What percentage of the points fall in each of the four quadrants? What do these percentages tell you about the association between the two variables?

Show your work.

Solution: _____

_____

_____

_____

_____

_____

Find the number of points in each quadrant and the total number of points on the graph. Then divide the number in each quadrant by the total number of points on the graph.

💬**Pair/Share**

What would the graph on the previous page look like if two of the quadrants contained 0% of the total number of points?

10 Which pair of variables would you expect to have a negative association?

A   The amount of money you make in a week and the number of hours you work during the week.

B   A person's height and the number of pets he or she owns.

C   The amount of money you have in the bank and the number of video games you buy.

D   The number of friends you have and the number of birthday parties you attend in a year.

Brian chose **B** as the correct answer. Why is Choice **B** incorrect?

_____

_____

_____

_____

You can often predict if a pair of real-world variables will have positive or negative association by thinking about the context.

💬**Pair/Share**

How would you help Brian understand his error?

Solve the problems.

1 Students at Central Middle School decided to gather survey data from their classmates on a number of different questions. Which pair of variables from the survey would be *most likely* to have no association with one another?

A number of hours spent studying per week and grade point average

B height in inches and age in months

C number of books owned and number of visits to the doctor's office in one year

D height and weight

2 The scatter plot below represents 2011 data comparing the average teacher salary and average student/teacher ratios for a number of school districts in the State of Vermont (source: education.vt.gov).

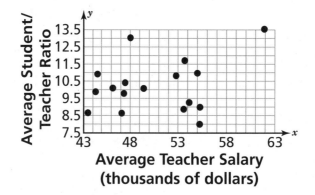

Choose True or False for each statement.

A An outlier exists at the point representing a salary of approximately $62,000. ☐ True ☐ False

B There is a negative linear association between average salaries and average student/teacher ratios. ☐ True ☐ False

C The smallest school district has an average student/teacher ratio of approximately 8.6. ☐ True ☐ False

D There is a positive linear association between average salaries and average student/teacher ratios. ☐ True ☐ False

E The school district with an average salary of $48,000 and a student/teacher ratio of 13 is an outlier compared to districts paying less than $48,000. ☐ True ☐ False

3 Each scatter plot below can be described by one of the following types of association.

Positive linear   Negative linear   Non-linear   None

Write the correct association below each scatter plot.

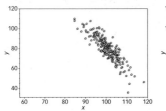 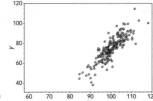 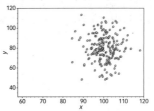 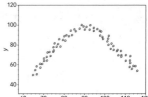

_____ _____ _____ _____

4 Invent your own set of bivariate data. Use the blank table and the scatter plot to both create and show your data. The data set should meet the following conditions:

• All *x*-values must be between 0 and 20; all *y*-values must be between 0 and 15.

• The association between the variables should be both negative and linear.

• One point should be an outlier; label that point "outlier."

Explain how your data set meets the above conditions by referring to specific features of the scatter plot and data set. Also provide an explanation for why the outlier exists in the data set.

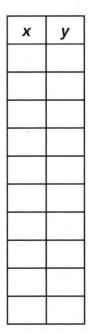 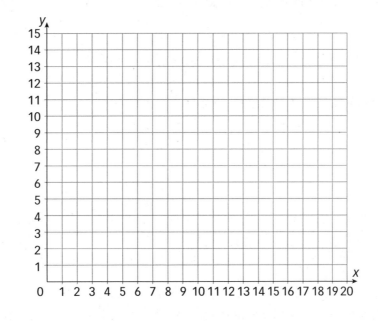

 **Self Check** *Go back and see what you can check off on the Self Check on page 239.*

Lesson 29   Part 1: Introduction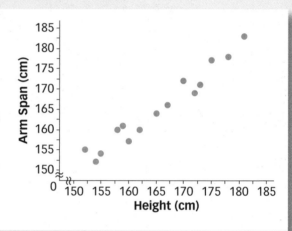

Scatter Plots and Linear Models

In the previous lesson, you learned how to analyze scatter plots. In this lesson, you will explore more tools that can help with scatter-plot analysis.

Students in an art class were learning to make realistic drawings of people. As part of their work, they investigated the relationship between height and arm span. They collected data from several individuals and made a scatter plot. Draw a line that best shows the trend of the data.

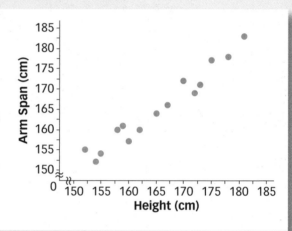

🔍 Explore It

Use the math you already know to solve the problem.

⬤ Sketch a line on the scatter plot that you think captures the trend of the data.

_____

_____

⬤ Explain how you decided where to place your line.

_____

⬤ Which points seem to be closest to the line? Which seem to be farthest?

_____

⬤ Take another look at the line you sketched earlier. Is it possible to improve it so there will be more points close to the line and fewer points far from it? If so, sketch the improved line. If not, explain why it is not possible.

_____

_____

_____

Find Out More

Many bivariate data sets have trends that can be described with straight lines. In the case of height and arm span, the points in the scatter plot show a positive association between the two variables. The data points are also close to falling along the same line.

In most statistical scatter plots, points will not all fall as close to the same line as they do in the height and arm-span plot. So, when placing a line in the scatter plot, aim to have the smallest possible total distance between the points in the plot and the line.

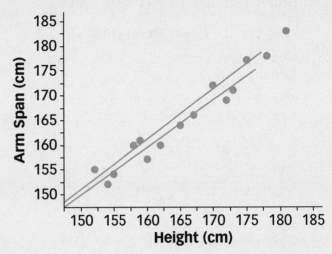

Here are two different trend lines. If you look at the points close to 160 on both axes, you'll see that one line is closer to the upper points while the other is closer to the lower points. The difference between the coordinates of points on the line and the actual points on the scatter plot are errors, or **residuals**.

You can't always eliminate error when fitting lines to data, but you can try to make the residuals as small as possible. Work to find a **best-fit line** that minimizes the distance between the actual data points and the line placed on the graph.

Reflect

1 Linear trends sometimes exist in bivariate data, but not always. On a separate piece of paper, draw a picture of a scatter plot for a data set where it would NOT make sense to try to fit a straight line to the data. On the lines below, explain why it would NOT make sense to use a straight line for the scatter plot you drew.

_____

_____

_____

_____

_____

Read the problem below. Then explore more about fitting a line to data to minimize errors in estimates with trend lines.

Paul and Joe placed their trend lines in a data set at different locations. The data set includes the following (x, y) ordered pairs: (1, 1), (2, 4), (4, 2), (5, 5), (8, 5). Whose line better captures the trend of the data?

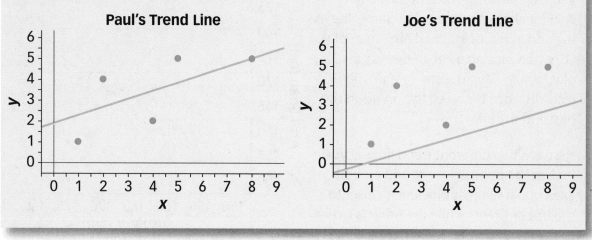

Model It

You can test the accuracy of a trend line by visualizing the residuals.

The trend lines Paul and Joe sketched both try to follow the trend, but they are positioned differently in relation to the points in the scatter plot.

To visualize the residuals for Paul and Joe's trend lines, you can insert vertical segments in the scatter plot.

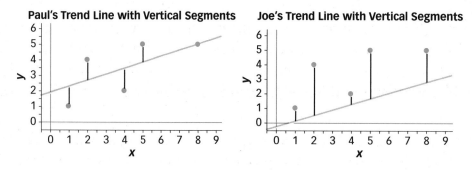

The vertical segments give an estimate of the distance between each point in the scatter plot and the two trend lines.

Connect It

Now you will decide which trend line is more suitable for the data set that Paul and Joe gathered.

2 Look at each trend line. Do you think Paul or Joe did a better job capturing the trend of the data? Explain.

_____

_____

3 Look at the vertical segments connecting each trend line to each of the data points. Estimate the length of each vertical segment in Paul's scatter plot, then add the lengths to find an approximate sum. Do the same with Joe's scatter plot.

_____

_____

4 Compare the sum of the vertical segment lengths in both graphs. How can this comparison help you decide which trend line is more suitable for the data?

_____

_____

5 Do the sums of vertical segment lengths support your answer to problem 2? Explain.

_____

_____

_____

Try It

Use what you just learned to solve this problem. Show your work on a separate sheet of paper.

6 Sketch a line on a grid. Place five data points to create a scatter plot in which the sum of the vertical segment lengths between the data points and the line is less than 1. How would you describe this situation?

_____

_____

_____

251

Outliers in bivariate data sets often pull trend lines in their direction.

☁Pair/Share

Give your own real-world example of a bivariate data set. Where might outliers come from in your data set?

Be careful about trying to fit a trend line to bivariate data. It doesn't always make sense to fit a trend line to all data.

☁Pair/Share

Do you think the data shown in the scatter plot are realistic? Why or why not?

Read the situation described below. Then solve problems 7–9.

Student Model

Mr. Finley drew two different trend lines for his data showing students' algebra test scores and time spent studying on the practice website. The first trend line accounts for the value that appears to be an outlier. This outlier was caused when one student logged into the wrong work station and added study time to the wrong person. Which trend line is better to use?

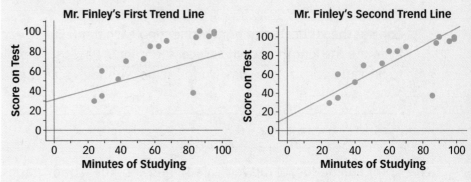

Solution: <u>Because an error caused the outlier, the second trend</u>

<u>line represents the data more accurately.</u>

7 This scatter plot shows students' algebra test scores and the time they spent studying on a different website. Do you think a trend line is appropriate for this data? Explain.

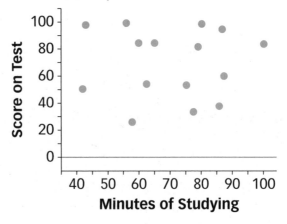

_____

_____

8 Mr. Finley is analyzing the data on students' algebra test scores and the number of texts they sent the day before the test. He puts the data in a scatter plot and is about to draw a trend line. What would a trend line show?

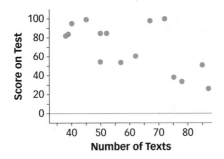

When fitting a line to a data set, keep the residuals as small as possible.

Pair/Share

Is a negative association the same thing as a zero association between variables? Why or why not?

9 Which scatter plot lends itself to having a trend line fit through the data?

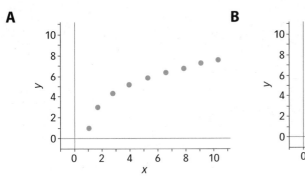

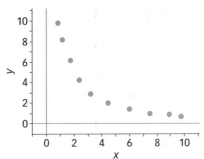

C neither scatter plot   **D** both scatter plots

Marnie chose **A** as the correct answer. How is the graph different from a linear trend with an outlier?

A line is just one kind of pattern in a scatter plot. Scatter plots can show lots of other patterns as well.

Pair/Share

How would you help Marnie understand her error?

Solve the problems.

1 Suppose two trend lines are sketched for the same data set in a scatter plot. How can you determine which of the two lines is the better fit?

 A determine which line is closest to the points in the scatter plot

 B determine which line is the steepest by finding out which one has the greatest slope

 C determine which line has the greatest *y*-intercept

 D determine which line intersects the *x*-axis closest to the origin

2 A teacher began collecting data for a particular test to see if an association exists between a student's time spent studying for the test and a student's test score. The data for most of her students is presented in the scatter plot below. A line of best fit shows the relationship.

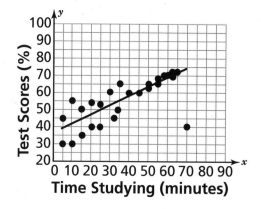

Choose True or False for each statement.

 A There is a negative association between study times and test scores. ☐ True ☐ False

 B The trend line predicts that a student who studies 80 minutes will get a test score of at least 75%. ☐ True ☐ False

 C The data values are more clustered around the trend line for study times of 40 minutes and higher. ☐ True ☐ False

 D The trend line predicts that a student who spends no time studying will get a 0% on the test. ☐ True ☐ False

 E The student who studied for 70 minutes but received a test score of 40 can be considered an outlier. ☐ True ☐ False

3 Invent your own 10-point set of bivariate data. List all the values in the data set in the table below and write a story to describe where you may have collected such data. Also produce a scatter plot for the data and a trend line. The data set should meet the following conditions:

- There should be a linear association between the two variables.
- The linear association should be negative.
- The sum of the distances from the data points to the trend line should be less than 10.

Story about where you collected your data: _____

_____

_____

_____

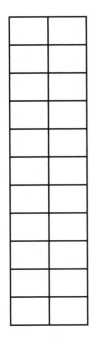

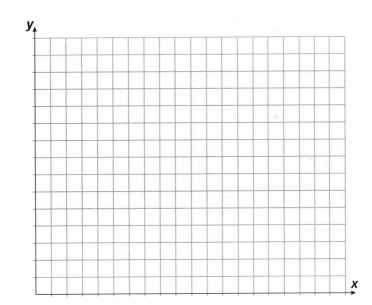

✓ **Self Check** *Go back and see what you can check off on the Self Check on page 239.*

CCSS
8.SP.A.3

Lesson 30   Part 1: Introduction 👥
Solve Problems with Linear Models

In the previous lesson, you learned how a line can be fit to data displayed in a scatter plot. In this lesson, you will explore how the equation of a line can help solve problems related to bivariate data sets.

Jenny recorded the height of the water in the bathtub as it drained after she pulled the plug. Her data is shown in the table and scatter plot. Write an equation to model the approximate height of the water over time.

Elapsed Time (sec)	Water Height (cm)
5	18.0
10	16.0
15	15.0
20	12.0
25	11.0
30	9.0
35	8.0
40	6.5
45	5.0
50	3.5
55	2.0
60	1.0

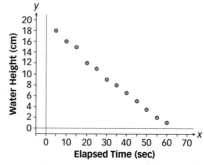

🔍 Explore It

Use the math you already know to solve the problem.

▪ Is the association between *x* and *y* positive or negative? Explain.

_____

▪ Is the association between *x* and *y* strong or weak in this case? Explain.

_____

▪ Sketch a line in the scatter plot to capture the trend you see in the data.

_____

_____

▪ Write the equation for your trend line in slope-intercept form.

_____

Find Out More

In lessons leading up to this one, you have sketched trend lines in scatter plots without writing their equations. Writing equations for trend lines can help you analyze data more deeply. Features of the equation such as its y-intercept and slope help you describe situations in greater detail.

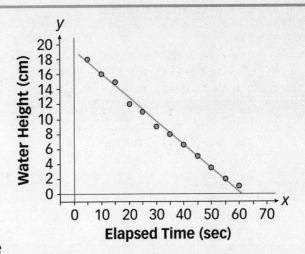

You know that the y-intercept is the value of y when x is equal to zero. This graph shows a possible trend line for the scatter plot on the previous page. The y-intercept of the trend line is approximately 19 cm. This gives an estimate of the height of the water in the tub when the elapsed time was zero, or the approximate height of the water in the tub before the plug was pulled. Jenny's data set did not show the exact height of the water in the tub to begin with, but the trend line and its equation help you make an educated guess.

The slope of the trend line also provides information. A positive slope indicates an uphill trend as you look from left to right. A negative slope indicates a downhill trend as you look from left to right. The slope also shows the change in the y-variable for each unit of change in the x-variable. The slope of the trend line in this graph is approximately -0.3. This means that the water level fell by about 0.3 cm each second after the plug was pulled in the bathtub.

The equation of the trend line also helps you make predictions.

Estimate the height of the water in the tub 17 seconds after the plug was pulled:	Estimate how long it took the tub to drain all of its water.
$y = -0.3(17) + 19$	$0 = -0.3x + 19$
$y \approx 15$ centimeters	$x \approx 63$ seconds

Reflect

1. Would it make sense to substitute an x-value greater than 70 into the trend line equation for the bathtub data? Would it make sense to substitute a y-value greater than 23 in the trend line equation for the bathtub data? Why or why not?

_____

_____

_____

_____

Read the problem below. Then explore more about how to use the equation for a trend line to analyze data.

Sandy surveyed her classmates to find the number of video games they owned and the number of hours they spent in front of the TV each week. She used a software program to find a line of best-fit for the data set she gathered. The data set and the output from the software are shown below. How can Sandy interpret the trend line that the software created?

Video Games Owned	Hours in Front of TV
1	10
1	14
2	14
3	15
3	17
4	20
4	15
5	20
6	20
6	23
7	24
8	26
9	27
9	25
10	28

hours in front of TV = h
video games owned = v
$h = 1.8v + 10.5$

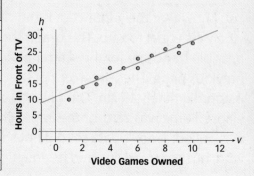

Model It

You can use horizontal and vertical lines from the x- and y-axes to help identify values.

The intersection of the horizontal and vertical lines provides an estimate of TV screen hours you might expect for someone who owned 4 video games. The y-value for $x = 4$ is about 17.5.

Substitute $x = 4$ in the best-fit line equation: $y = 1.8 \cdot 4 + 10.5 = 17.7$.

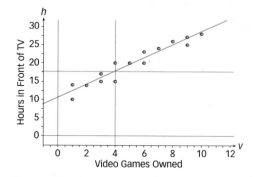

Model It

To examine the slope of the best-fit line equation, determine the increase in y as x increases by 1.

The horizontal and vertical dotted segments along the best-fit line graph show the x and y increases. Each time an x-value increases by 1, the corresponding y-value increases by 1.8.

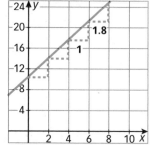

Connect It

Now you will use these representations to solve problems.

2 No one in Sandy's survey said they owned 11 video games. Use the graph on the previous page to estimate the number of hours someone who owned 11 video games would spend in front of the TV each week. Explain how you made your estimate.

_____

_____

_____

3 Substitute $x = 11$ in the equation for the best-fit line. What y-value do you get? How does it compare to your answer for problem 1?

_____

4 Explain the meaning of the slope of the best-fit line as relates to the number of video games owned and the amount of time spent in front of the TV each week.

_____

_____

5 Explain where the y-intercept is represented on the graph and in the equation for the best-fit line. What is the y-intercept?

_____

_____

Try It

Use what you just learned about equations for best-fit lines to solve this problem. Show your work on a separate sheet of paper.

6 Explain how you would interpret the value of the y-intercept in the context of the problem.

_____

_____

_____

When fitting a trend line to data, try to get the smallest possible total distance between the data points and the line itself.

Read the situation described below. Then solve problems 7–9.

Student Model

Several stores in Centerburg sell 24-stick packs of Juice-Yum Gum. The stores charge different prices. They also sell different numbers of packs per month, as shown in the data and scatter plot.

Write an equation for a trend line that does a good job capturing the trend of the data.

Price per Pack ($)	Pack Sold per Month
2.75	201
2.80	197
2.85	195
2.95	192
3.10	186
3.12	185
3.20	181
3.23	175
3.25	168
3.36	165
3.40	162
3.40	157
3.55	151
3.60	144
3.75	136
3.76	133
3.90	128
3.93	121

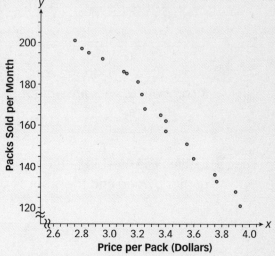

Pair/Share

Why do you need just two points in order to write the equation of a line?

Solution: One reasonable trend line goes through the points

(2.95, 192) and (3.55, 151). The slope is $\frac{151 - 192}{3.55 - 2.95} = -68.\overline{3}$. To

find the *y*-intercept, solve the equation $192 = -68.\overline{3}\,(2.95) + b$

for *b*; $b \approx 393.5$. So, the approximate trend line equation is

$y = -68.3x + 393.5$.

If you know the x-value, how can you use the equation to find the corresponding y-value?

Pair/Share

Do trend line equations give you exact predictions or do they give estimates? Defend your position.

7 A new store in Centerburg plans to sell packs of Juice-Yum for $3.65 each. Use the trend line equation to give an estimate of the number of packs per month they are likely to sell.

_____

_____

_____

8 What is the *y*-intercept in the equation of the trend line in the student model? Explain what the *y*-intercept means in the context of the problem. Do you think it has a useful interpretation?

Solution: _____

_____

_____

_____

_____

If the y-intercept of a trend line is far away from most of the data points in the scatter plot, it is likely that it does not have a useful interpretation.

💬 **Pair/Share**

How do you find the *y*-intercept if you are given the equation of a line in slope-intercept form? How do you find the *y*-intercept if you are given a graph?

9 Which is the most reasonable interpretation of the slope of the trend line in the student model?

A The slope has no meaningful interpretation in this situation.

B The slope means you can expect to lose about 68 gum-pack sales per month for every one dollar price increase.

C The slope means you can expect to sell about 393 packs of gum if you drop the price to zero dollars.

D The slope indicates there is a positive association between the price charged per pack and the number of sales you can expect to make.

Jack chose **C** as the correct answer. How did he get that answer?

_____

_____

_____

When interpreting the slope, think about what "change in y for each one unit increase in x" means for the data set.

💬 **Pair/Share**

How would you help Jack understand his error?

Solve the problems.

1 George and Martha go to different schools. Each collected data on students' heights (*h* inches) and weights (*w* pounds) at their own schools. For their respective data, they each drew a line of best-fit and determined its equation. They then compared equations and made inferences based only on the equations they calculated.

Student	Equation of Trend Line
George	$w = 6.22h - 250.67$
Martha	$w = 5.94h - 232.24$

Decide whether you agree or disagree, based only on the equations above, with the inferences drawn by George and Martha.

A George states that the students that he surveyed weigh more, on average, than the students Martha surveyed. ☐ Agree ☐ Disagree

B Martha states that her trend line suggests that for every 1-inch decrease in height, there is a decrease of 232.24 pounds in weight. ☐ Agree ☐ Disagree

C George states that his trend line indicates that for every 6.22-inch increase in height, there is an increase of 1 pound in weight. ☐ Agree ☐ Disagree

D George says that his equation's intercept of negative 250.67 has no relevant meaning since negative weights are not possible in the real world. ☐ Agree ☐ Disagree

E Martha states that for every 1-inch increase in height, there is a 5.94-pound increase in weight. ☐ Agree ☐ Disagree

2 Suppose you know that one student in George's data set weighs 150 pounds. What would the trend line equation in Problem 1 predict for the student's height, to the nearest inch?

A 401 inches

B 251 inches

C 6 inches

D 64 inches

3 Invent your own set of bivariate data that has a linear association. List all the values in the data set in a table and describe where you might have collected such data. Also produce a scatter plot for the data and a trend line. Then do the following:

- Write the equation for the trend line you sketched.

- Explain the meaning of the slope within the context of your data set.

- Explain the meaning of the *y*-intercept within the context of your data set.

- Make at least one prediction using the trend line equation and its graph.

Be sure to explain your reasoning completely and show all of the work you did to complete each task.

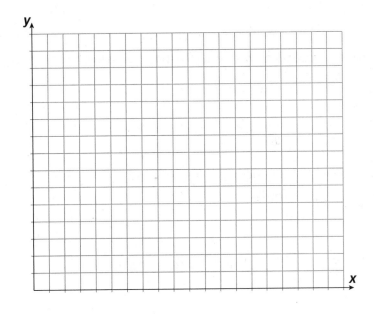

_____

_____

_____

_____

_____

_____

_____

✓ **Self Check** *Go back and see what you can check off on the Self Check on page 239.*

Lesson 31   Part 1: Introduction 👥

Categorical Data in Frequency Tables

CCSS

8.SP.A.4

In previous lessons, you learned how scatter plots can be used to analyze bivariate quantitative data. In this lesson we will explore techniques for analyzing bivariate categorical data.

Alexander took a poll of 8th and 12th grade students in his school district. He was interested in whether or not students in these grade levels owned a tablet computer. He gathered the data shown in the table. What relationships can he find?

🔍 Explore It

Use the math you already know to answer the question.

Respondent	Grade	Tablet?
1	8	yes
2	12	yes
3	8	no
4	12	no
5	12	yes
6	8	no
7	8	no
8	12	yes
9	8	yes
10	8	no
11	12	no
12	8	no
13	12	no
14	8	yes
15	12	yes
16	8	yes
17	8	yes
18	12	yes
19	12	no
20	8	no
21	12	yes
22	8	yes
23	8	yes
24	8	no
25	12	no
26	12	yes

- How many eighth graders were surveyed? How many own tablet computers?

  _____

- How many twelfth graders were surveyed? How many of them own tablet computers?

  _____

- What percentage of twelfth graders surveyed own a tablet?

  _____

- What percentage of eighth graders in the survey own a tablet?

  _____

- Do the data suggest that there is a relationship between grade level and tablet ownership? Explain.

  _____

  _____

  _____

Find Out More

Your work so far with bivariate data has focused on looking for relationships between quantitative variables, for example, time spent studying vs. score on a test. Scatter plots are convenient tools for analyzing these types of situations because the ordered pairs in the scatter plot contain information about two quantities that can be shown on the *x*- and *y*-axes of a graph.

Scatter plots do not work when all data are not numbers. Some data sets include **categorical data** and consist of category labels rather than numbers. For example, in the survey of eighth and twelfth graders, one of the variables is tablet ownership. There are just two possible values for this variable: "yes" and "no." The other variable is grade level. The values for this variable are "eighth grade" and "twelfth grade." Since these grade levels are category labels, they are considered categorical even though the category labels can be represented with numerals.

Without using a scatter plot, you can still analyze the data to see if there is a relationship between tablet ownership and grade level in school. You might conjecture, for example, that twelfth grade students are more likely to own tablets than eighth graders. To test that conjecture, you could compute the percentage of students at each grade level who reported owning tablets, as shown on the previous page.

Percentages are usually more valuable than raw frequencies when examining relationships between categorical variables. In the tablet survey, the same number of eighth graders and twelfth graders reported owning tablets. Just looking at those raw frequencies, you might draw the conclusion that tablet ownership does not depend on grade level. However, the percentages suggest a different story. Since there were fewer twelfth graders taking the survey, the percentage of them who owned tablets was slightly higher.

Because it is such a small sample, we cannot draw any definitive conclusions about association. However, if we continued to gather data and these percentages held up, we might reasonably assume that twelfth graders are more likely to own tablet computers. This would suggest that there may be an association between the categorical variables of grade level and tablet computer ownership.

Reflect

1 Give two of your own examples of categorical variables. Explain why it would not be possible to display the variables in a scatter plot.

_____

_____

_____

Read the problem below. Then explore how to look for association between two categorical variables.

> Angela wondered if there was an association between gender and favorite color, so she conducted a survey of students in her school. Of the girls responding to the survey, she found that 33 preferred blue, 8 brown, 7 green, 10 orange, and 25 pink. Of the boys responding to the survey, she found that 60 preferred blue, 10 brown, 12 green, 16 orange, and 26 pink.

 **Model It**

You can display the results of the survey in a two-way table.

	Favorite color					
	Blue	**Brown**	**Green**	**Orange**	**Pink**	**TOTAL**
Female	33	8	7	10	25	83
Male	60	10	12	16	26	124
TOTAL	93	18	19	26	51	207

Two-way tables provide a way to summarize data on two categorical variables collected from the same population of individuals. This two-way table shows the frequency of each favorite color among boys and girls in the survey. The column totals show how many students in all had each favorite color. The cell in the bottom right shows the total number of survey respondents.

Model It

You can also use two-way tables to display the percentage of each favorite color among boys and girls in the survey.

	Favorite color				
	Blue	**Brown**	**Green**	**Orange**	**Pink**
Female	39.8%	9.6%	8.4%	12%	30.1%
Male	48.4%	8.1%	9.7%	12.9%	21%

This type of two-way table shows **relative frequencies** across the rows. That is, it shows how common each favorite color was in comparison to the others for each gender. Note that percentages in the rows do not necessarily add to 100% because of rounding to the nearest tenth.

Connect It

Now you will use the two-way tables from the previous page to solve problems.

2 Describe the calculations Angela did to get the percentages shown in the second table.

_____

_____

3 Would you say the data shows that boys and girls had an equal preference for pink? Explain.

_____

_____

_____

4 What is the difference in percentages for girls and boys for each favorite color?

_____

_____

5 Look at your answer for Problem 4. Do you think that there is an association between gender and color for any of the favorite colors? Explain.

_____

_____

_____

_____

Try It

Use what you just learned about data in two-way tables to solve this problem.

6 Seventh graders were asked if they get an allowance and if they do chores. Does the data here support the idea that those with an allowance are more likely to do chores? Explain.

	Allowance	No Allowance
Chores	61	32
No Chores	42	22

_____

_____

Read the situation described below. Then solve problems 7–9.

Two-way tables can be left in terms of raw frequencies if you just want to examine the grand totals of participants in a given category.

Pair/Share

What information would you get if you added down each column instead of adding across each row?

Each column represents a different region of the country, so you can compute percentages down each column to compare regions.

Pair/Share

When does it make sense to compute relative frequencies down columns? Across rows?

Student Model

Workers at a large company took part in a voluntary survey about the political party they support. Results are shown in the table.

	Region of U.S.				
	Northeast	**Southeast**	**Midwest**	**Southwest**	**West**
Democrat	37	15	22	31	42
Republican	12	25	19	26	12
Independent	5	7	9	6	7

How many Democrats, Republications, and Independents took part in the survey?

Solution: __To determine the number of people for each political__

__party, calculate the row totals. There are 37 + 15 + 22 + 31 +__

__42 = 147 Democrats. There are 12 + 25 + 19 + 26 + 12 = 94__

__Republicans. There are 5 + 7 + 9 + 6 + 7 = 34 Independents.__

7 Does the data provide evidence that a worker's political party is associated with the region of the country in which he/she lives? Build a relative frequency table to support your response.

_____

_____

_____

_____

_____

8 What is the probability of selecting a Democrat at random from the employees in the Southeast? Is it the same as the probability of randomly selecting someone from the Southeast when sampling from Democrat employees? Explain.

Solution: _____

_____

_____

_____

_____

Row totals and column totals can be helpful when computing probabilities.

💬 Pair/Share

Name several other probabilities you can compute from Mike's data.

9 Which region of the country has the greatest percentage of employees who are Republicans?

A Northeast

B Southeast

C Midwest

D Southwest

Millie chose **D** as the correct answer. Why is her answer incorrect?

_____

_____

_____

_____

Be careful not to confuse raw frequencies with relative frequencies.

💬 Pair/Share

How would you help Millie understand her error?

Solve the problems.

1 The table below displays data on a survey asking a group of car owners to report the type of car they drive and their income level. Each survey respondent owned just one car.

	Type of Car				
	Compact	**Mid-size**	**Full-size**	**Luxury**	**TOTAL**
Low income	34	22	15	7	78
Middle income	28	38	30	10	106
High income	10	25	27	37	99
TOTAL	72	85	72	54	283

What percentage of middle-income earners owned compact cars?

A   38.9%

B   26.4%

C   9.9%

D   28%

2 Caroline asked 100 students in 9th grade whether they prefer chocolate ice cream or vanilla ice cream and whether they prefer chocolate sprinkles or rainbow sprinkles. Given the following information, complete the table by writing a number in each empty cell. Choose from the given multiples of 5.

65% of the students prefer chocolate ice cream.
45% of the students prefer rainbow sprinkles.
30% of the students prefer both vanilla ice cream and rainbow sprinkles.

5	10
15	20
25	30
35	40
45	50
55	60
65	70

Sprinkles	Ice Cream		**TOTAL**
	Chocolate	Vanilla	
Chocolate			
Rainbow			
TOTAL			100

3 Based on the information in Problem 2, which statement is a valid inference? Select all that apply.

A Of those surveyed who like vanilla ice cream, more than 85% prefer rainbow sprinkles.

B Of those surveyed who like chocolate ice cream, fewer than 25% prefer rainbow sprinkles.

C If a student from those surveyed is chosen at random, the probability that the student prefers both chocolate ice cream and chocolate sprinkles is $\frac{1}{2}$.

D If a student from those surveyed is chosen at random, the probability that the student prefers both vanilla ice cream and chocolate sprinkles is $\frac{1}{6}$.

4 Does the table in problem 1 support the idea that there is an association between an individual's income level and the type of car they drive? In justifying your response, use relative frequencies when appropriate.

_____

_____

_____

_____

_____

_____

_____

_____

_____

 **Self Check** *Go back and see what you can check off on the Self Check on page 239.*

Solve the problems.

1 In a survey, citizens of Joss and Kath Counties were asked whether they voted "yes" or "no" on building a new courthouse. The table shows the results.

Vote	Joss	Kath	Total
Yes	15	58	73
No	26	9	35
Total	41	67	108

To the nearest percent, what percent of all "no" votes came from Kath County?

A 13%   **C** 26%

B 16%   **D** 35%

2 Look at the following scatter plot.

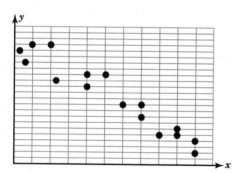

Which could be the equation for the line of best-fit? Select all that apply.

A $y = \frac{5}{2}x - \frac{9}{5}$

B $y = -0.03x + 81.357$

C $y = -8.25x + 150$

D $y = -\frac{2}{3}x - \frac{10}{3}$

E $y = -25x + 1,000$

3 Data is collected from 20 students. They are asked whether or not they have a curfew on school nights and do chores at home. Choose four numbers from those given below to complete the table. Make sure the following conditions are met.

- The number of students who do chores is less than the number of students who do not do chores.

- The number of students who have a curfew is less than the number of students who do not have a curfew.

- The association between having a curfew and doing chores is that students who have a curfew tend to do chores, while students who have no curfew tend not to do chores.

		Curfew	
Chores		Yes	No
Yes			
No			

1
2
3
6
9

4 A taxi-cab service charges its customers based on an initial, fixed fee and a per-mile rate. The equation $c = 2.5m + 5$ models this situation, where c is the total cost of a ride and m is the number of miles traveled.

Part A

Identify the values of the slope and the y-intercept in this equation.

Answer _____

Part B

In words, explain what the slope and the y-intercept stand for in this real-world situation.

_____

5 The math and reading teachers in a school were asked whether the school should buy 10 new computers for the computer lab. Their responses are shown below.

Vote	Math Teachers	Reading Teachers	Total
Yes	5	12	17
No	9	7	16
Total	14	19	33

Part A

Of the math teachers, what percent voted **against** buying the new computers? Round your answer to the nearest percent.

Show your work.

Answer _____

Part B

Of all the teachers who voted **for** buying the new computers, what percent are math teachers? Round your answer to the nearest percent.

Show your work.

Answer _____

Performance Task

Answer the questions and show all your work on separate paper.

Ned, the owner of *Everything Electronic*, took a survey of customers in the store one Saturday morning. The table below summarizes the data collected.

Ned has given you the job of analyzing the survey data so he can learn more about his customers. In browsing through the data, Ned thought there might be a relationship between a customer's age and the number of apps they downloaded last month.

☑ **CHECKLIST**

Did you . . .

☐ Draw a graph?

☐ Use a graph to analyze the data?

☐ Answer all the questions asked?

Shopper	Gender	Age	Number of apps downloaded last month	Brand of tablet
1	Male	8	3	E-Tablet
2	Male	12	5	Blueberry
3	Male	11	4	E-Tablet
4	Male	9	4	E-Tablet
5	Male	8	2	Blueberry
6	Female	10	6	Blueberry
7	Female	13	7	Blueberry
8	Male	14	6	Blueberry
9	Male	22	5	Blueberry
10	Female	8	4	E-Tablet
11	Male	11	4	Blueberry
12	Female	15	8	Blueberry
13	Male	16	10	E-Tablet
14	Male	11	5	Blueberry
15	Female	13	6	Blueberry
16	Male	16	9	Blueberry
17	Female	12	6	E-Tablet
18	Female	10	5	Blueberry
19	Female	14	8	E-Tablet
20	Male	9	5	E-Tablet
21	Male	17	9	Blueberry

A. Construct a scatter plot to display these two variables. Describe any patterns you see.

B. Draw a best-fit line for this data and describe it with an equation. How can Ned use this line to make predictions and help with business decisions?

Reflect on Mathematical Practices

After you complete the task, choose one of the following questions to answer.

1. **Be Precise** Is the *y*-intercept of your line a possible data point for the data that Ned collected? Explain.
2. **Reason Mathematically** Are there any points on your graph that don't fit with the rest of the data points? Did this affect how you drew your line?

The chart below correlates each Common Core State Standard to the *Ready® Common Core Instruction* lesson(s) that offer(s) comprehensive instruction on that standard. Use this chart to determine which lessons your students should complete based on their mastery of each standard.

Common Core State Standards for Grade 8 — Mathematics Standards		Content Emphasis	Ready® Common Core Instruction Lesson(s)
The Number System			
Know that there are numbers that are not rational, and approximate them by rational numbers.			
8.NS.A.1	Know that numbers that are not rational are called irrational. Understand informally that every number has a decimal expansion; for rational numbers show that the decimal expansion repeats eventually, and convert a decimal expansion which repeats eventually into a rational number.	Supporting/ Additional	3
8.NS.A.2	Use rational approximations of irrational numbers to compare the size of irrational numbers, locate them approximately on a number line diagram, and estimate the value of expressions (e.g., π^2). *For example, by truncating the decimal expansion of $\sqrt{2}$, show that $\sqrt{2}$ is between 1 and 2, then between 1.4 and 1.5, and explain how to continue on to get better approximations.*	Supporting/ Additional	3
Expressions and Equations			
Expressions and Equations Work with radicals and integer exponents.			
8.EE.A.1	Know and apply the properties of integer exponents to generate equivalent numerical expressions. *For example, $3^2 \times 3^{-5} = 3^{-3} = \frac{1}{3^3} = \frac{1}{27}$.*	Major	1
8.EE.A.2	Use square root and cube root symbols to represent solutions to equations of the form $x^2 = p$ and $x^3 = p$, where p is a positive rational number. Evaluate square roots of small perfect squares and cube roots of small perfect cubes. Know that $\sqrt{2}$ is irrational.	Major	2
8.EE.A.3	Use numbers expressed in the form of a single digit times an integer power of 10 to estimate very large or very small quantities, and to express how many times as much one is than the other. *For example, estimate the population of the United States as 3×10^8 and the population of the world as 7×10^9, and determine that the world population is more than 20 times larger.*	Major	4
8.EE.A.4	Perform operations with numbers expressed in scientific notation, including problems where both decimal and scientific notation are used. Use scientific notation and choose units of appropriate size for measurements of very large or very small quantities (e.g., use millimeters per year for seafloor spreading). Interpret scientific notation that has been generated by technology.	Major	5
Understand the connections between proportional relationships, lines, and linear equations.			
8.EE.B.5	Graph proportional relationships, interpreting the unit rate as the slope of the graph. Compare two different proportional relationships represented in different ways. *For example, compare a distance-time graph to a distance-time equation to determine which of two moving objects has greater speed.*	Major	11
8.EE.B.6	Use similar triangles to explain why the slope m is the same between any two distinct points on a non-vertical line in the coordinate plane; derive the equation $y = mx$ for a line through the origin and the equation $y = mx + b$ for a line intercepting the vertical axis at b.	Major	12

The Standards for Mathematical Practice are integrated throughout the instructional lessons.

©2010. National Governors Association Center for Best Practices and Council of Chief State School Officers. All rights reserved.

Common Core State Standards for Grade 8 — Mathematics Standards	Content Emphasis	Ready® Common Core Instruction Lesson(s)
Expressions and Equations (*continued*)		
Analyze and solve linear equations and pairs of simultaneous linear equations.		
8.EE.C.7 Solve linear equations in one variable.	Major	13, 14
8.EE.C.7a Give examples of linear equations in one variable with one solution, infinitely many solutions, or no solutions. Show which of these possibilities is the case by successively transforming the given equation into simpler forms, until an equivalent equation of the form $x = a$, $a = a$, or $a = b$ results (where a and b are different numbers).	Major	14
8.EE.C.7b Solve linear equations with rational number coefficients, including equations whose solutions require expanding expressions using the distributive property and collecting like terms.	Major	13
8.EE.C.8 Analyze and solve pairs of simultaneous linear equations.	Major	15, 16, 17
8.EE.C.8a Understand that solutions to a system of two linear equations in two variables correspond to points of intersection of their graphs, because points of intersection satisfy both equations simultaneously.	Major	15
8.EE.C.8b Solve systems of two linear equations in two variables algebraically, and estimate solutions by graphing the equations. Solve simple cases by inspection. *For example, $3x + 2y = 5$ and $3x + 2y = 6$ have no solution because $3x + 2y$ cannot simultaneously be 5 and 6.*	Major	16
8.EE.C.8c Solve real-world and mathematical problems leading to two linear equations in two variables. *For example, given coordinates for two pairs of points, determine whether the line through the first pair of points intersects the line through the second pair.*	Major	17
Functions		
Define, evaluate, and compare functions.		
8.F.A.1 Understand that a function is a rule that assigns to each input exactly one output. The graph of a function is the set of ordered pairs consisting of an input and the corresponding output.	Major	6
8.F.A.2 Compare properties of two functions each represented in a different way (algebraically, graphically, numerically in tables, or by verbal descriptions). *For example, given a linear function represented by a table of values and a linear function represented by an algebraic expression, determine which function has the greater rate of change.*	Major	7
8.F.A.3 Interpret the equation $y = mx + b$ as defining a linear function, whose graph is a straight line; give examples of functions that are not linear. *For example, the function $A = s^2$ giving the area of a square as a function of its side length is not linear because its graph contains the points (1,1), (2,4) and (3,9), which are not on a straight line.*	Major	8
Use functions to model relationships between quantities.		
8.F.B.4 Construct a function to model a linear relationship between two quantities. Determine the rate of change and initial value of the function from a description of a relationship or from two (x, y) values, including reading these from a table or from a graph. Interpret the rate of change and initial value of a linear function in terms of the situation it models, and in terms of its graph or a table of values.	Major	9
8.F.B.5 Describe qualitatively the functional relationship between two quantities by analyzing a graph (e.g., where the function is increasing or decreasing, linear or nonlinear). Sketch a graph that exhibits the qualitative features of a function that has been described verbally.	Major	10
Geometry		
Understand congruence and similarity using physical models, transparencies, or geometry software.		
8.G.A.1 Verify experimentally the properties of rotations, reflections, and translations:	Major	18
8.G.A.1a Lines are taken to lines, and line segments to line segments of the same length.	Major	18
8.G.A.1b Angles are taken to angles of the same measure.	Major	18
8.G.A.1c Parallel lines are taken to parallel lines.	Major	18

The Standards for Mathematical Practice are integrated throughout the instructional lessons.

Common Core State Standards for Grade 8 — Mathematics Standards		Content Emphasis	*Ready®* *Common Core* *Instruction* Lesson(s)
Geometry (*continued*)			
Understand congruence and similarity using physical models, transparencies, or geometry software. (*continued*)			
8.G.A.2	Understand that a two-dimensional figure is congruent to another if the second can be obtained from the first by a sequence of rotations, reflections, and translations; given two congruent figures, describe a sequence that exhibits the congruence between them.	Major	19
8.G.A.3	Describe the effect of dilations, translations, rotations, and reflections on two-dimensional figures using coordinates.	Major	19, 20
8.G.A.4	Understand that a two-dimensional figure is similar to another if the second can be obtained from the first by a sequence of rotations, reflections, translations, and dilations; given two similar two-dimensional figures, describe a sequence that exhibits the similarity between them.	Major	20
8.G.A.5	Use informal arguments to establish facts about the angle sum and exterior angle of triangles, about the angles created when parallel lines are cut by a transversal, and the angle-angle criterion for similarity of triangles. *For example, arrange three copies of the same triangle so that the sum of the three angles appears to form a line, and give an argument in terms of transversals why this is so.*	Major	21, 22
Understand and apply the Pythagorean Theorem.			
8.G.B.6	Explain a proof of the Pythagorean Theorem and its converse.	Major	23
8.G.B.7	Apply the Pythagorean Theorem to determine unknown side lengths in right triangles in real-world and mathematical problems in two and three dimensions.	Major	24
8.G.B.8	Apply the Pythagorean Theorem to find the distance between two points in a coordinate system.	Major	25
Solve real-world and mathematical problems involving volume of cylinders, cones, and spheres.			
8.G.C.9	Know the formulas for the volumes of cones, cylinders, and spheres and use them to solve real-world and mathematical problems.	Supporting/ Additional	26, 27
Statistics and Probability			
Investigate patterns of association in bivariate data.			
8.SP.A.1	Construct and interpret scatter plots for bivariate measurement data to investigate patterns of association between two quantities. Describe patterns such as clustering, outliers, positive or negative association, linear association, and nonlinear association.	Supporting/ Additional	28
8.SP.A.2	Know that straight lines are widely used to model relationships between two quantitative variables. For scatter plots that suggest a linear association, informally fit a straight line, and informally assess the model fit by judging the closeness of the data points to the line.	Supporting/ Additional	29
8.SP.A.3	Use the equation of a linear model to solve problems in the context of bivariate measurement data, interpreting the slope and intercept. *For example, in a linear model for a biology experiment, interpret a slope of 1.5 cm/hr as meaning that an additional hour of sunlight each day is associated with an additional 1.5 cm in mature plant height.*	Supporting/ Additional	30
8.SP.A.4	Understand that patterns of association can also be seen in bivariate categorical data by displaying frequencies and relative frequencies in a two-way table. Construct and interpret a two-way table summarizing data on two categorical variables collected from the same subjects. Use relative frequencies calculated for rows or columns to describe possible association between the two variables. *For example, collect data from students in your class on whether or not they have a curfew on school nights and whether or not they have assigned chores at home. Is there evidence that those who have a curfew also tend to have chores?*	Supporting/ Additional	31

The Standards for Mathematical Practice are integrated throughout the instructional lessons.